Trust and Mistrust:
Radical Risk Strategies in
Business Relationships

Trust and Mistrust

Radical Risk Strategies in Business Relationships

Aidan Ward
and
John Smith

WILEY

Copyright © 2003   John Wiley & Sons Ltd, The Atrium, Southern Gate, Chichester,
West Sussex PO19 8SQ, England
Telephone (+44) 1243 779777
Email (for orders and customer service enquiries):
cs-books@wiley.co.uk   *Call*
Visit our Home Page on www.wileyeurope.com or www.wiley.com

This publication is designed to provide accurate and authoritative information in regard
to the subject matter covered. It is sold on the understanding that the Publisher is not
engaged in rendering professional services. If professional advice or other expert
assistance is required, the services of a competent professional should be sought.

Other Wiley Editorial Offices
John Wiley & Sons Inc., 111 River Street, Hoboken, NJ 07030, USA
Jossey-Bass, 989 Market Street, San Francisco, CA 94103–1741, USA
Wiley-VCH Verlag GmbH, Boschstr. 12, D-69469 Weinheim, Germany
John Wiley & Sons Australia Ltd, 33 Park Road, Milton,
Queensland 4064, Australia
John Wiley & Sons (Asia) Pte Ltd, 2 Clementi Loop #02–01,
Jin Xing Distripark, Singapore 129809
John Wiley & Sons Canada Ltd, 22 Worcester Road, Etobicoke,
Ontario, Canada M9W 1L1

Wiley also publishes its books in a variety of electronic formats. Some content that
appears in print may not be available in electronic books.

Library of Congress Cataloging-in-Publication Data
Ward, William Aidan.
    Trust and mistrust: radical strategies in business relationships/
William Aidan Ward and John Robert Smith.
        p. cm.
    Includes bibliographical references and index.
    ISBN 0-470-85318-2 (cloth: alk. paper)
    1. Strategic alliances (Business)   2. Trust.   3. Business ethics.
    4. Organizational effectiveness.   I. Smith, John Robert.   II. Title.
    HD69.S8W37 2003
    650′.01–dc21   2003007461

British Library Cataloguing in Publication Data
A catalogue record for this book is available from the British Library

ISBN 0-470-85318-2

Typeset in 11/13 Goudy by Florence Production Ltd., Stoodleigh, Devon
Printed and bound in Great Britain by TJ International Ltd., Padstow, Cornwall

This book is printed on acid-free paper responsibly manufactured from sustainable
forestry in which at least two trees are planted for each one used for paper production.

Contents

Preface

This has been a difficult book to write. When I consider why I think the issue is this. There is an expectation that, in a business book, ideas are put forward with supporting evidence about how those ideas produce better business outcomes than their supposed rival ideas. When the book goes out to review or I imagine the reader reading it, I have to deal with that expectation.

The expectation contains two problems. First, it is distrustful in its nature and this book is about the effects of trust not of distrust. Second, it uses a notion of business outcomes that we hope to show is self-limiting if not self-defeating. The outcomes we want trust to deliver are not on this map, although secondary effects of trust are clearly visible in the bottom line.

That such a book can get written is already a minor miracle of trust. We are particularly grateful to Diane Taylor at John Wiley, who trusted us to produce a business book that deals with something that is not supposed to be an issue in the business world: the accountability of people for the nature of their relationships with others.

The challenge to the reader is this: can you exercise critical thinking not to dismiss the arguments of the book but to open up new questions about business practice and business potential? We have persevered with the project because there is an audience of business readers who particularly need an insight into why the predominant approaches to business relationships and to building or recovering trust are so unsuccessful.

In the political life of the UK the effects we talk about in the book are writ large as we write this and probably determine the future of the government. There is a determined and long-term attempt by governments of both persuasions to improve the value for money spent on public projects and services. The Treasury sets performance targets and establishes schemes such as the Private Finance Initiative to reduce costs and export risk to agencies and contractors. The available evidence, much of it necessarily anecdotal and private, is that this has greatly increased costs and escalated risk to the public purse. It is difficult to imagine a more contentious issue, but from the perspective of this book the multiple distrust of the Treasury (of the agencies and contractors, of the public in its need for evidence, of other government departments etc.) actually leads directly and inevitably to huge avoidable costs and risks. For the record it appears that the US situation is recognizably similar.

Our argument is that it is necessary to take the immediate personal and political risk of trust and engagement with the other players, and accept that this creates vulnerability for both sides. By avoiding this fundamental first step and hiding behind mechanisms, contracts and legal provisions, what has actually been hidden is the ways in which all those mechanisms can be exploited. It was ever thus, but the lesson has to be learnt anew by each generation. For the first time, to our knowledge, we explain here how the trust equations produce this inevitable result. The way we relate to others in our business dealings determines the nature of the options open to us. Low-trust ways of relating are incredibly constraining of those options, even while they appear to give defensive security.

Likewise in business organizations, certainly the many we have worked with, there is doing the business and there is demonstrating what a good job you are doing. If the latter is done in a spirit of mistrust, doing the business is damaged 90% of the time. Accountability for this effect, which is larger than other performance factors, is non-existent. The people we work with can generally describe (and lament) this effect from their personal experience. They know it to be the experience of their peers also. But they cannot see a way through. If this is your experience, then this book is for you. People are not in general cynical, but the systems we work in certainly are.

However, although we as authors keep succumbing to the temptation to describe the mess people get into, the message of the book is elsewhere. The message is how to understand the types of trust necessary to do the business, and how to manage the risk involved in extending that trust.

W.A.W.
Longfield
26 November 2002

To me there are three vital issues as far as trust is concerned. First is understanding what it is. I get this understanding through the model Aidan and I have developed. Second is doing something about it (if I choose to). This ability – that great feeling of being able to change something as a result of knowing something or learning something – comes through use of the Scimitar methodology we have developed together over a number of years. It is a privilege to get the opportunity to share these understandings with the reader.

The third issue is that the first two have to apply to every aspect of my life regardless of situation and context. Of the three this is the most important to me.

The opening sentence of our introduction is *We all know what trust is* and of course we do, just as we all know what food is or travel or well-being or music or management. One of the things *we all know* about all those things (and practically everything else in our lives) is that there are hundreds of books about them and hundreds of experts ready to give us advice and tell us what's what about them. Trust isn't like that. Trying to describe the taste of a raspberry, for example, is really a waste of time. Pop one into your mouth and try. Trust is like that. As the great Ludwig Wittgenstein said, 'no one can think a thought for me just as no one can don my hat for me'.

We already knew that our Scimitar methodology worked in the wider world – that it wasn't constrained solely to managing business risk – and our trust model needed to be in keeping. My view is that it does precisely this. I see our model as the equivalent of the old machine code in computing. It underpins the whole shooting match. Everything else – languages, operating systems, utilities, applications, communications channels, user interfaces, you name it – all run on it and are all compiled under it.

Leaders and managers have sometimes to drill down as far as they can go. I think dealing with trust is one of those times. When you get there you'll find our model.

J.R.S.
Beighton
22 November 2002

Glossary

Lots of reading has been done and lots of ideas explored by the authors during the time it took getting this book from concept to hardback. Our annotated bibliography and guru list is a brief distillation of that work. The hope is that in reading it the reader will get two things from it. The first is a sense of precisely how densely interconnected the world is (and the connotations this has for business improvement). The second is that by 'standing on the shoulders of giants' we all get a better view of whatever it is we are looking at.

There are several – no more than a dozen or so – key ideas and concepts that are impossible to present other than in their original words. While their meanings are explained in the text and bibliography, the glossary below provides a shorthand guide.

Amputation Marshall McLuhan's insight that technological improvements, while extending our capabilities in some way, cause the skills that are made redundant in doing so to be amputated.

Authenticity The difference between a person applying his or her skills to the achievement of a task and a person creatively working for success is authenticity.

Commoditization The change that takes place when something that was once special and scarce becomes a mere thing of trade.

Consistent The fact that some of our feelings about what motivates us to trust are fairly unchanging in the short term. Given our nature, authentic trust and authority trust tend to be consistent. An exploitable source of leverage in the power game.

Device paradigm Albert Borgmann's brilliant exposition of the nature and impact of commoditization.

Degrees of freedom The scientific and mathematical notion that there are independent directions in which progress is possible.

Extension McLuhan's upside to his downside amputation.

Inconsistent The fact that some of our feelings about what motivates us to trust can change rapidly and are likely to do so. Network trust and commodity trust tend to be inconsistent. An exploitable source of leverage in the power game.

POSIWID Acronym reflecting the fact that the purpose of a system is what it does.

Publicness The loss of the authentic self that arises from conformance with imposed preconceptions, options and values.

Reification The process by which we convert people into things and things into people to make dealing with them more comfortable for ourselves.

Scimitar Risk management system designed, developed and owned by Antelope Projects, forming the direct bridge between the abstract world of trust and the real world of business improvement.

Unencumberment Describes the way our lives are made easier with commoditization. Similar to McLuhan's concept of extension.

An Introduction
to Trust

We all know what trust is. We know it instinctively and intuitively. Our knowledge of it is in many ways more useful and more practical than the descriptions of it in the literature. Our knowledge informs the ways we relate to others, including the ways we do business. Since time immemorial and never more than today, we need to know who we can trust with what. We want to draw out and build on that intuitive knowledge.

Trust affects power. It changes the balance of power in relationships. Trust between people increases security and potential while it lasts. Trust produces the vulnerability to the risk of betrayal and failure. In some of the modes of trust we will describe, trust is associated with power to influence, power to manipulate, power to exploit and even, *in extremis*, the power to dominate. These effects of trust in modulating the power balance across business relationships are less well understood. They need to be articulated if we are to understand how to extend trust. In many ways business language hides these effects: we are often uncomfortable describing business as the exercise of power, and even more uncomfortable talking about accountability in the use of power.

We want to reclaim a meaning of risk closely associated with the exercise of power. If we trust someone we put ourselves at risk but we do so voluntarily. There may be no way to get a piece of business done except to engage with that personal risk. To deny or externalize that risk is to start to enter the world of blame and the misuse of power. We want to reconnect our intuitive understanding of trust with a sense of the roots of business risk.

In our business dealings we have little difficulty extending this understanding. We know when we trust another organization or another division of our own organization, and we know the sorts of things that can put that trust under strain. We probably say that trust is important in business and that to build trust is to build a foundation for business success.

There are, however, things that confuse our instinctive understanding of trust:

- When there is a formal process or bureaucratic procedure involved in our dealings with an organization we lose sight of the object of trust: do we trust the process, the operator of that process or the institution that owns the process?
- When we are looking for a service and the requirements we have are not met by the available offerings: do we trust the providers of the offerings?
- When someone whose integrity we believe in has to make a pronouncement in public about some fraught subject: do we trust the information he or she conveys?

All these scenarios have a business context where the logic of the context and the logic of trust are at odds with each other. And, business being what it is, countless others arise endlessly. Understanding trust in a full business context is much more demanding than understanding it in simple relationship terms. The aim throughout this book is to enable the reader to reach an understanding of trust and to plot a course for improvement by modelling and analysing all the factors that are at work. We then show how the resulting trust analysis is used in delivering and managing these improvements in the real world in which the firm has to exist.

A model should be as simple as possible and no simpler. Our model of trust extends our instinctive understanding to distinguish four different sorts of trust and their interaction. By starting to classify the different sorts of trust important in business situations we can see more clearly both how to build appropriate trust and how to manage the business risks involved.

The Importance of Trust in Business Environments

With good enough trust between the parties in a business environment, you can:

- be aware of far more of the workings of the environment, including how you can generate value for other stakeholders;
- strengthen business relationships to deal with unimagined opportunities and contingencies;
- understand how to develop lean business processes without unnecessary or counterproductive management activities;
- manage business risks that will otherwise play havoc with the business.

Something about the way that businesses and business sectors are organized and the business cultures they create leads to a lack of appreciation of the potential in this list. Today when the word trust is on everyone's lips there is little or no systematic discussion of its importance for today's business decisions. Our aim is to fill the gap by describing how to build appropriate business trust and how to get that trust to build into sustainable business advantage. Trust is, of course, all about sustainability anyway.

A Cycle of Abuse

When business people deny the importance of trust, when some of their business relationships become cynical and exploitative, then a cycle is formed: lack of trust leads to cynical actions and cynical actions lead to a further erosion of trust. People come to discount anything that is said and instead look for evidence of devious ulterior motives. A firm with responsibility for maintaining the safety and serviceability of the UK rail network extended this cycle into the realms of double-bluff by refusing to discount sabotage as the cause of a fatal accident despite there being no evidence to that effect.

In a number of recent cases – for instance, Enron, Worldcom, Xerox and Railtrack – we have seen the public face of business drift well away from its underlying state. This is not a new problem: we well remember BCCI, Barings Bank and the Maxwell affair. Nor are these isolated cases of criminality in a sea of upstanding business behaviour. All businesses, including our own, learn to present themselves in a way that furthers their business interests. If there is a problem here it is as much the public fantasy – that there are straightforward 'facts' to be 'disclosed' – as it is to do with deliberate business disinformation. There is every bit as much of a problem with people acting on partial information without context to the detriment of a business's interests as there is a problem with businesses being economical with the business truth.

As an example, consider safety critical software in modern aircraft. Many software systems are critical to the safety of an aircraft and the public have some awareness of this. The public face of the industry is that this software does not have errors that could cause its failure: people simply would not fly. Engineers recognize that this Holy Grail of error free software has never been achieved and is never likely to be.

A colleague of ours who demonstrated his software quality toolset on a 'live' sample of this software reported so many problems that he thought he had been given some test code designed to exercise all aspects of his toolset! It is difficult to hold together the public face and the private reality: no one would publish an article we wrote exploring this difficulty. Indeed, the public face very much gets in the way of improving the quality of the software. Boeing, to give it credit, when it set up the project team for the software intensive 777 actually tackled this cultural problem head on. The public perception of these issues is always likely to be misguided. We could recall the Ariane 5 rocket, which used tried and tested navigation software from Ariane 4. It crashed because the greater acceleration of Ariane 5 took some numbers in the software beyond their limits, causing the programmed destruction of the rocket. The Airbus Industrie approach to software, in vicious competition with Boeing, emphasizes separation between software and aeronautics, as did Ariane. Despite events, the public perception is that this is nevertheless an advantage.

What we see in this example and in the major failures quoted is simply business risk in operation. There is no doubt that all businesses in all their business relationships have to negotiate these sorts of problems. With shareholders, suppliers, customers, regulators and staff there is a balance to be struck between presentation and manipulation, between trying to engage stakeholders in the substance of the issues they face and making space for corrective action un-impeded by unhelpful investigation.

The crucial link in these delicate (or gross!) negotiations of business risk is trust. Can the other parties be trusted to play a posi-tive role if disclosure takes place? When the UK government intervened to sort out the mess Railtrack had made of the rail infra-structure, they arguably made the problem much worse by seeming to overstep the bounds of trust. Trust encompasses not only belief in good intentions but in competence and other knock-on effects. It is not surprising that in many instances businesses choose to keep their own counsel and hope for better times around the corner. And it is not surprising that often those better times do not arrive.

The Power and Trust Dilemma

As a general observation, there are two ways to get business action: you can build collaboration with other stakeholders or you can push things through. The use of power to push things through can generate an addictive pattern of behaviour for organizations (Figure 1).

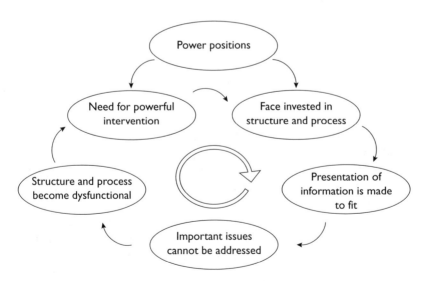

Figure 1 Power positions are self-stabilizing regardless of outcomes

This diagram illustrates quite clearly how the 'sabotage' issue in rail maintenance referred to above can become the firm's instinctive response, leaving the true cause of the problem unaddressed. Within this system people with power are always 'right' because there will always be a need for them to step in to rescue the immediate situation. The behaviour becomes addictive and so perpetuates the cycle. Again, trust is needed to allow a management situation to stabilize and become effective. Counter-intuitively, trust is needed for power solutions to work as other than purely political moves. The majority of management solutions generally only 'work' in this political sense and so in fact add to the problems they purport to solve. This is the root of the spectacular failures we have noted and many more mundane crises as well.

Our work as researchers and consultants has led us to the following observations:

- most people can see these sorts of systemic failures in situations they are not directly involved in, but cannot see them when they are too close;
- the cultures of the organizations we work with rarely support dialogue about systemic failures such as addictive behaviour;
- all organizations progressively lose the ability to ask the questions that count most.

Of course, as researchers and consultants we ourselves are not immune from these effects. In particular, it is a tough challenge to communicate at all about issues that are plain to us and at the same time strangely invisible to business people we would like to help as clients.

What we put forward is a model of how trust works in a business world. We explain how, by building the types of trust needed in a particular situation, addictive behaviour and spurious management initiatives can be avoided. We have come to believe that only by understanding how to build capability in this way can the underlying problems be seen. So the format of the book is to explain the importance of the different types of trust and to explain how they can be used to manage business risk. By following this programme we hope readers will discover for themselves business risks they are currently systematically blind to. This need not be enigmatic: once you have built trust with some stakeholders, they will certainly tell you some things you never suspected!

There is also a positive benefit statement available from the perspective of lean systems. (A lean system is both effective and efficient because it has been progressively stripped of activities that do not add value to its purpose – for example, the Toyota Production System). From the perspective of appropriate trust in the key business relationships it is possible to see which activities, and in particular which management activities, are unnecessary or counterproductive.

Trust in Business

For the first time in almost half a century, the question of whether business corporations can be trusted, of whether businesses can deliver on what they promise, is firmly on the public agenda. Businesses too have questions about their business environment: can they trust the accounts of auditors? Can they trust the major providers of software systems? Can they trust their customers?

There have been shocks to the overall system of commerce that have brought these questions of trust to the fore. There have been major food scares that have given rise to doubt about the safety of what is on our plates. There have been corporate and market collapses that have suddenly destroyed people's savings. There have been entire industries transferred from public to private ownership with little or no consideration given to trust implications. There have been admissions that trade policies are rigged in favour of the rich and powerful. There have been transport scandals in the UK that have resulted in people doubting the authorities' commitment to public safety. There have been terrorist outrages that raise questions about foreign policy and the unilateral imposition of values. Most of us do not have to deal with these events directly in our businesses, but all of us experience the secondary effects in a changed business climate. In particular, there is more automatic scepticism and less immediate trust.

In all these cases people make pronouncements about the need to rebuild trust, about how our way of life depends on trust, about how business relies on its infrastructure of commercial relationships. Our particular subject here is the effectiveness of these pronouncements and programmes that are supposed to build trust: too often they seem to have the opposite effect to that intended. Businesses need to know how to evaluate the trust they already use and rely on. They need to know what can damage it and what it takes to repair it. They need to know what they could achieve if they trusted more. They need a model of trust that is more use to them in developing strategy and tactics, in choosing a business path.

What Is Trust?

In developing our working definition of trust we begin with this simple statement:

> To trust is to rely on someone or something to take care of our interests.

To trust is not to assess trustworthiness. Neither is trust blind to risk and the possibility of betrayal. It is not a cost-free option. To trust is an act, a business move, which has profound consequences. It is radical in the sense that there is no substitute for it and its consequences and implications are unavoidable.

Our working definition talks about taking care of our interests. A major issue that we will have to confront is whether those interests can be assumed, or whether they are particular and specific to us. One major reason for the failure of trust is being treated indifferently, as though we were no different to anyone else. This one-size-fits-all lack of understanding of difference causes us to question whether we and our business have any distinct significance that is comparable to the trust we have extended. Trust is human and our uniqueness as individuals and business players is one reason why trust is radical in its implications.

This is the simplest trust scenario: two individuals simply trying to understand the degree to which they can rely on each other rather than establishing detailed expectations of each other's behaviour, or, heaven forbid, a contract. One fascinating question cannot be avoided any longer: is the world that one individual sees the same as the world the other sees? This is a bit philosophical but desperately important: the notion of where a person's interest lies is dependent not only on the particular issue at hand but on the context of that issue. For example, whether a business deal is in my interest or not depends crucially on judgement about the character of the people in that deal. Now, we could shape this concern as a problem, that the person I want to trust might not see the same set of 'facts' as I do, but actually this is a major opportunity for trust, as our developing definition makes clear:

> Trust in someone allows us to extend our awareness to things that person can see that we cannot.

We can readily understand the thrust of this: if someone else can see something I cannot see, is their awareness centred on their own interest or on mine? We all see what we want to see to some degree: does this person see just what they want to see or does that 'wanting' encompass my interest as well? And take the inverse of this: I am to some extent blind to things that are unacceptable to me. Another person I trust does not suffer from these same blind spots and can therefore bring these things to my awareness. But how are they to introduce me to these things I do not want to know? Only by my trust in their handling of my best interests. Trust is never easy.

There is also a process angle on trust. How do I get to trust someone? This has a chicken and egg feel to it because until I extend trust I cannot experience a person's response to that trust, and until I experience the response I may feel unable to trust. Because this is a business book and because we take a radical view we are going to work with the proactive proposition: I extend trust because that is what I choose to do. We will explore at length why this cannot be a utilitarian choice – I choose to trust because it will lead to other things I want – but for now we need merely to insist that trust is not about an assessment of trustworthiness:

> The choice of trust in another party is not subject to pre-conditions.

If we make statements like 'I would trust you if only you could do this or not do that' we are making nonsense of the word. Equally if we say, 'I can demonstrate my trustworthiness in this way and so you should trust me' we are also making a nonsense. If we want preconditions then we are trying to hedge our trust, trying to bolster our judgement and hence muddying the act of trust. And that is what we have contracts for.

The process angle on trust also leads us to ask about the path of trust and its growth or diminishment. Conventional wisdom is that trust takes a long time to grow, perhaps decades if we are talking about societies, but that it can be lost overnight. Our view is a little different. If trust is built cynically and then that cynicism is exposed then of course trust is lost overnight. We might think of the Ratner debacle where the much-admired chief executive of the jewellery chain told his business fans that he sold junk. The basis on which his trust was built crumbled with his revelation and with it his empire. That said, there are also studies that show that trust often starts high and then is consolidated or eroded as the case may be. If we choose to trust and if we take care not to expose fledgling trust to more than it can bear then there is no reason why adverse events, which to a suspicious mind might lead to a questioning of the choice of trust, cannot lead to a strengthening and reinforcing of trust. These are real choices and they lead to different outcomes if we commit to them.

So not only is the initial choice of trust not sensibly subject to preconditions, but the continuance of the path has a similar struc-ture:

> Any event in a relationship can be used to enhance or diminish trust depending on the choices the parties make.

Clearly, however, if the relationship event is that the cynicism of one party is exposed, then real change is necessary if trust is to be enhanced.

To return to the public face of business, our initial question is this:

> If a business is explicitly organized to meet the needs of its shareholders, why, not being a shareholder, would I believe that it will take care of my interests?

This question is repeatedly raised around businesses that have implica-tions for public safety such as the railways and air traffic control, but other domains generate the same question: I have financial interests, ethical interests, political interests, social interests etc., all of which can be harmed by a business that does not take care of them. Trust is about all these things, though we are certainly conditioned not to expect certain sorts of interest to be taken care of by businesses.

Businesses must concern themselves with levels of trust in all their stakeholder relationships: customers, suppliers, employees, regulators etc. Indeed, from a trust perspective it is the quality of these relationships that facilitates or inhibits the business in achieving anything it sets out to do.

Different Types of Trust

Throughout this book we distinguish four different types of trust that have different properties. To establish the differences, look at the four different ways we might trust an organic food supplier:

(1) The food has been produced according to the letter of the regulations. Buying such food is to trust the institutional regulation of the term 'organic' and the producer's compliance.
(2) The food is sold using organic as a 'brand' label and has been bought from the cheapest producer, often with the weakest or least enforced regulations. Buying such food is to trust the supplier not to jeopardize the brand by actually cheating.
(3) The food is produced locally or down at the allotment with plenty of muck and no sprays. Buying such food is to trust the local community and a relationship with someone whose food values you agree with.
(4) The food is the product of a movement that cares about the environment and about customers ahead of profits and intensive practices. Buying such food is to trust the power of a set of community values to enable self-policing of production standards.

The business relationships embodied in these four different sorts of trust are different and to some extent mutually exclusive. When we have contradictory ideas about what trust rests on and what it implies then it is very easy for a programme designed to build (rebuild) trust to backfire. If I want to promote sustainable agriculture and I believe that my supermarket's pricing policy erodes organic standards, then whether their produce complies with the letter of the regulation is neither here nor there. Not surprisingly, the reasons why we want to trust are as important as the reasons that businesses want to be trusted.

These different sorts of trust can also be described as different assumptions about the sort of environment in which trust can be sustained and can grow:

(1) *Authority trust*: only a completely consistent and reliable mode of service delivery can be trusted to give me what I need every time.
(2) *Commodity trust*: only a mode of service delivery which is explicitly and dynamically tuned in to customer demands can be trusted to supply what I actually need.
(3) *Network trust*: only by listening to the experiences of friends and acquaintances can I understand what I need and avoid being duped.
(4) *Authentic trust*: only by extending trust can I create an environment in which the service delivery I need is made possible.

Once again, we will not manage to build trust if we fail to pay attention to the different assumptions people are working with. Colin Powell, the US Secretary of State, addressing the World Summit in Johannesburg, South Africa in September 2002, effectively offered the world's poorest people the stark choice between starvation and eating the same genetically modified produce that Americans eat. 'Trust us,' he seemed to be saying, 'it's for your own good and it hasn't done us any harm'. We cannot, however, command trust, no one can force it to appear, nor even buy it: if we want trust we must deal with where people are and we must apply leadership to generate new possibilities.

The Economic Impact of Trust

To understand the economic impact of trust as a factor in the business environment, we must focus on the nature of business relationships. In particular, we must focus on the need for stable cooperation in relationships. Can relationships be sustained as long-term win–win propositions for all parties to them?

Many people still assume that stable cooperation can be generated by establishing the appropriate contractual framework. Experience appears to show that while contracts have an important role, they are not good foundations for relationship development. What is so difficult about business relationships that they require more than contractual commitment? We need to answer this question from the following three important perspectives:

(1) Is the contractual commitment genuine?
(2) What unforeseen risks may change the situation?
(3) What exists as a shadow side of the contract?

Contractual commitment may be tactical rather than genuine. In practice a contract is as much something to hide behind and avoid saying things, as it is something to base a comprehensive agreement around. There is always a larger game than the contract envisages in which the contract is itself a pawn. Take, for instance, a good candidate who signs an employment contract with a company solely for the experience and training it will bring him, knowing he will be able to move to a competitor company at a better salary as a result. Although both sides may have dealt with this possibility in their own way, there is a gap between the spoken purposes and the unspoken purposes.

Where contractual commitment is essentially the result of a power imbalance between the parties (they almost always are), sooner or later the externals of the situation will change and allow the weaker party to take revenge. Typically, large external risks have this effect, changing the conditions envisaged in the contract so that non-cooperation is damaging to the more powerful party. Take, for instance, a supplier who has had a consignment of goods returned on specious quality concerns because it did not suit the purchaser to meet the contractual conditions when too much had been ordered. What is going to happen when there is a sudden shortage and this supplier is left holding the cards?

Like all human affairs, a contract lives in public (although secret contracts are possible), and so has a shadow side of motivation that is denied, or simply beyond awareness. Motivations we can think of as being positive drivers towards some more or less clear objective. The shadow side can give rise to equally powerful drivers towards some alternative or unstated objective. Blindness to the shadow is a driver of Murphy's Law that anything that *can* go wrong *will* go wrong. As such, it is a significant though often overlooked component of risk management. Trying to bring commitment to an explicit agreement without trust in the underlying relationships creates all sorts of unexpected effects that have their roots in the unacknowledged motivations. If we think about the job candidate and his employment contract, we can observe how little of the real implications of employment is ever discussed at interview or during selection. The shadow side is a source both of problems and of strength: we know that by denying, repressing or ignoring shadow-side issues they will come back to haunt us but it is also true that by trusting our darker and more intuitive side we can find real power and creativity. Murphy's Law can guide us to a really lean process.

Trust is the ground from which we can tackle all these issues. If we have trust across the relationships concerned then either or any party can bring up issues that need to be addressed for mutual benefit. Without trust it may be literally true that it is not safe to talk about particular issues. Over time the relationships will not survive if it is not possible to talk through issues before they do their damage. This allows us to extend our definition of trust:

> Trust is that ability of the parties to a relationship to raise and deal with issues that may otherwise damage it.

There is always a risk in raising difficult subjects. Messengers have, after all, been known to have been shot. We do not know in advance how another person or business will respond to our insights and our concerns. Raising the issue at an inappropriate time may ultimately be as damaging as not raising it at all. It may be our perspective that is inappropriate rather than the issue being a serious concern. We cannot ever know with certainty. Whether we are dealing with issues of motivation, of risk, or of the shadow side, we need something to give us confidence that we can invest in the relationship by taking the risk.

This issue of trust may be local and kept private from wider systems or it may involve, by implication, other parties and other systems. When someone raises an issue that they think can be sorted out in a particular relationship, it may bring some other relationship into question in a way they had not anticipated. Trust is an attribute of relationships but we live in complex webs of interdependency and it is highly unlikely that islands of trust can long survive in a cultural sea of suspicion.

The Economics of Getting Trust Wrong
The UK construction sector has a fragmented and conflict-ridden supply chain. The supply chain is both broad, with a wide range of general and specialist functions supplied by different companies, and deep, with many sub-contracts and sub-sub-contracts to the nth degree. These companies bid for contracts with a tight profit margin, perhaps as low as 3%, and an expectation that when the contract needs to be changed they can make a better margin on the resulting work. This approach is resented and resisted by companies putting work out to tender, who try to pass on risk and cost to the bidders.

In a government-sponsored report, Sir John Egan pointed to waste in the supply chain running at more than 40% of overall costs. A large component of this waste is all the activity of setting up and policing contracts and then suing for costs incurred in doing extra work and counter-suing for work not done according to contract. The roots of this waste lie in extreme mistrust between the companies involved, and the universal opinion that the contract system must be used to achieve a reasonable return on work done and to avoid the costs of risk and change. All this is well understood and extensively documented.

The UK government is a major construction customer, to the tune of £67 bn each year. The size of the potential payoff, on its own figures, for avoiding some of the waste in the supply chain is colossal. The government also has a substantial stake in the global competitiveness of the UK construction industry. Tellingly, however, government investment in the schemes set up to address the issue of waste is minuscule, something below 0.01% of the potential payoff.

This is not simply an economic issue. The safety record of the industry is very poor and the law is being changed to allow the Health and Safety Executive (HSE) to prosecute construction (and other) firms and their directors. Charges will relate to management systems falling below what could be expected in protecting the safety of workers on construction sites. When projects get late, people have more accidents. When work is concentrated into hot spots, people have more accidents. For the record, we do not believe these legal moves will improve safety.

We have mentioned the schemes set up to address these problems, structured as clubs of enlightened companies who want to improve their margins by avoiding some of the waste. Though these clubs have had some success, that success remains marginal in terms of the sector as a whole. There is a proof of concept, if you like, but no change. So we are looking at a sector that systematically reproduces:

- a production process that is wasteful, gives poor quality results and often late delivery;
- a set of working practices that gives high accident rates, both fatalities and serious injuries;
- a contractual system where disputes are the norm and adjudication is needed just to keep it running;
- an organizational environment that everyone finds stressful and unrewarding.

Developing a Trust Model that Works

Trust in Context

Context is everything when it comes to trust. So developing a radical trust model that works – that is, one that does practical and useful business work whatever the context – has meant drawing on lots of disciplines that business book readers mostly try to avoid, like philosophy, sociology, systems theory, game theory, psychology, economics and such.

That said, and by way of a little context setting, we have set out (as part of our bibliography under the heading 'Gurus you can trust and ideas you can use') a brief guide to some of the thinkers whose work has influenced the production of this book and some of the ideas from which the model was derived. For the busy manager investing time, energy and tolerance in a business book we feel this is an important grounding.

(Also, the thing with great thinkers and gurus is that their world of ideas is about precisely that – ideas. Once a notion is in the public domain it is available for whatever anyone wants to make of it, including developing radical business strategies. Whatever the context, copyrighting ideas is always a trust-blocking device. Einstein had no copyright on his general theory; neither did Keynes or Plato on theirs. Step changes in knowledge come from insights – the one per cent inspiration that leads to the ninety-nine per cent perspiration follow-up. It is available to us all.)

Dimensions of Trust

There is no single issue of 'trust'. Someone might think it OK to trust if certain safeguards are in place, and not if not. The business and management challenge is how to engender trust within a given set of people, in a given set of circumstances and thereby improve business performance. And trust, as we have seen, is not some soppy, touchy-feely niceness aimed at countering the cynicism of worldliness. It is about hard, and hard-nosed, decisions.

Trust is by no means a new challenge, of course. It has been known about for centuries. And the challenge in that time has been met with some impressively innovative solutions. Among the best of these is the pledge given by his eighteenth-century noblemen to the king of Aragon:

> We, who are as good as you, acknowledge you, who are no better than us, to be our sovereign lord ruling over us, providing you respect our laws and traditions. And if not, not.

Sets of people and sets of circumstances are countless and ever changing, making management akin to trying to build on shifting sand. Trust itself though, fortunately for the future of management science, has the four easily identified dimensions we referred to earlier. These are the backbone of our book. Understanding them is a key to success. The dimensions have been best described, by Professor Bernard Williams, as the drivers that motivate us to cooperate for some collectively desired outcome. Given a business-focus, they form the basis of this book's trust model. Balancing them enables trust to be managed. In classic four-box diagram form, Williams's motivators to cooperate are as shown in Figure 2, with our trust types added in bold.

	Macro	Micro
Egoist	**Authority trust** Fear of sanction Imposed choice	**Authentic trust** Self-interest Personal choice
Non-egoist	Moral, religious or ethical disposition to cooperate – a sense of duty or responsibility **Commodity trust**	Family ties, friendly relations and a willingness to cooperate **Network trust**

Figure 2 Williams's motivators to cooperate

In this model, macro motivations can be thought of as motivations we have 'in general' – motivations that arise 'as often as not'. Micro motivations are more contextual, more dependent on the circumstances and groups we find ourselves in.

Egoistic motivations, as the name implies, are based more closely on personal perceptions than are non-egoistic motivations. These latter represent perceptions we share with groups we belong to. The power that non-egoistic motivations have over situations we find ourselves in leads to many of business-life's paradoxes. We explore some of these in detail throughout the book.

Trust Space Mapping: The Dimensions of Trust

Relationships are impossible without trust. And, since business is impossible without relationships, it follows that business itself is impossible without trust. That said, the true nature of the trust that underpins business is often poorly understood. Equally often, where there is some understanding, its true nature is denied, or covered up by something more commercially convenient or else subverted into something more politically acceptable. Derived from Williams's four-box diagram, the model in Figure 3 uses the four types of trust as dimensions or horizons to map the space within which relation-

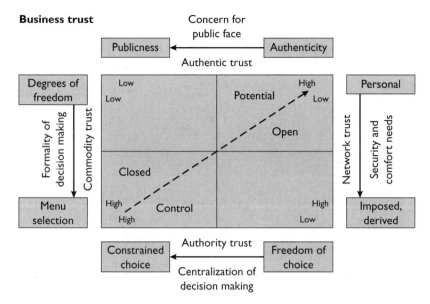

Figure 3 The dimensions of business trust

ships and organizations have to live and business transactions have to take place. It shows the connections between the different sorts of trust and the issues raised as a result. When they are used as dimensions, their influence ranging from low to high, the various types of trust look like this.

Trust is choice. And, as with any choice we ever make, trust comes at a cost. And where there is cost there is risk. Every choice we make implies that there are alternative choices we have discarded. Economists refer to these forgone choices as opportunity cost (we think of them as opportunity risk). The model illustrates the opportunity risk of choosing to trust. In doing so it paints a clear picture of the risk that accompanies that choice. (The point has already been made that risk can only be managed once it is taken. Otherwise it remains entirely notional. Later in the book we show how we bridge the gap between the notional world of the model and the real world where business risk exists and has to be managed.)

That said, the essential message of the model is that trust is always available and its cost is always fully assessable and always fully understandable in terms of its implicit risk. By implication a better (more productive, more profitable and probably in the short term, more risky) trust position is always available above and to the right of the present position. The rest of this book is structured around the model's dimensions where they are explored in detail. Below they are set out by way of an introduction.

- *Authentic trust.* An absence of authentic trust implies having an overriding concern for public appearance and a conformance to the requirements of that appearance. The word that describes this concern is publicness. As authentic trust grows, and publicness reduces, so focus shifts towards a genuine expression of personal choice and a pursuit of self-interest which is to a great extent indifferent to the views of others and is based upon personal achievement, an openness and honesty that is neither rude nor lacking in consideration.
- *Network trust* reflects our need for comfort and safety. Low reliance on network trust gives rise to the self-containment and adherence to personal values that characterize authentic behaviour, whereas a high level of reliance indicates acceptance of imposed or derived values. This is where the 'jobsworth' is to be found.
- *Authority trust* reflects our degree of willingness to submit to hierarchies, in particular hierarchies where decisions are taken centrally. Essentially, the more we submit, the more choices we indicate we are prepared to forgo and the more of our options we allow to be closed off, and vice versa.
- *Commodity trust* essentially concerns the formality and the nature of the forces at the heart of the decision-making process. Generally speaking, the higher the formality, the more constrained the set of choices we have available and, again, vice versa. Brands and bureaucracies live largely in this dimension.

Two important issues need to be borne in mind using these dimensions. The first is that no single dimension determines behaviour on its own. And the dimensions themselves make certain mutually exclusive trust positions clear from the outset. For instance, a high requirement for authority trust and/or commodity trust implies high levels of network trust and a high degree of publicness. Similarly, concern for public face and reputation and a centralized style of decision making will preclude potential for innovation and openness to future possibilities. In trust terms the model explains the crucial differences between the bureaucrat and the entrepreneur, and between the traditional firm and the innovators.

We use the map throughout the book, examining each dimension in turn not merely for its characteristics as a type of trust but, more significantly, for the role it plays in conjunction with the others in improving business performance.

The logic of the map, as has already been said, is that there is always an improved position available to the right of and above the present situation. The challenge then becomes, first, understanding where that improved position is located and, second, getting there. These are the challenges the book addresses.

The Roots of the Model

Management started the day business itself started. Experts and 'how to do it' gurus, bristling with their latest books, came following close behind. Business schools started shortly afterwards and in no time flat business itself became big business. It has stayed that way, a market growing inexorably with no sign of letting up.

One of my references assures me that an eighteenth-century Italian academic called Antonio Genovesi was the first person to ever hold a chair of commerce at a university, Naples University in this instance. So he can claim to be business's first acknowledged expert, its first voice of authority, its first guru. Today, without even bothering to count them, it is easy to imagine the world has tens of thousands of these such experts, any one of whom is capable of telling us, in the minutest detail, precisely where old Antonio went wrong, what he really should have done back then and what he would need to do to cut the mustard today.

Nowadays, by means of this process, experts – Genovesi's successors – are the established owners of the conventional wisdom of business and management. As managers, our relationships with them are as much based on trust as any others so it is worth looking briefly at the basis of that trust. Experts own the past and all its towering figures and its great thinkers. Part of their role is to bring the lessons of the past into the present in the hope of influencing the future. Their key to doing this lies in summarizing knowledge – turning it into a commodity – delivering the benefits of laborious study while freeing us from the hassle of actually having to do the laborious study for ourselves. As a result we trust them. To a large extent they determine what is and what isn't acceptable. (So much so that I am practically spooked by even mentioning Genovesi, let alone calling him by his first name, for fear of getting 'how dare you' emails from his fan club. It will get worse when I draw from other greats and even worse than that when I draw parallels with game theory and other models of how the world works. In fact I've started already. The term 'conventional wisdom', slipped in above, although nowadays part of everyone's vernacular, was coined by the great twentieth-century economist John Kenneth Galbraith in his 1958 book, *The Affluent Society*. Conventional wisdom describes ideas so ingrained nobody ever questions them. We use this book to explore the implications of trusting conventional wisdom.)

Living with Business

So while experts can tell us everything about everything to do with management whether we're in oil, insurance, local government, retailing, leisure, market gardening or selling solar panels over the internet, the truth is that in practice things are a little different. Nobody is very long in management without becoming familiar with the cyclical nature of business. The fact is we live it. At some remove we have all studied marketing's famous product life cycle model and at some remove we are all familiar with the cyclical nature of our own careers, our own mortality and the lives of those we love and who depend on us. Crucially in this context, we all understand the precise connections between flavours and months.

Conventional life-cycle wisdom has it that experts live forever in that guruic zone around which all emergent knowledge comes out while the rest of us inhabit that mortal plateau of baseness known as the 'real world'. Sooner or later, thanks to some poorly understood osmotic process, the real world gets to take the new knowledge on board and life becomes richer for everyone. Underneath it all, the cycle perpetually and seamlessly renews itself.

There are at least two problems with this though. First, thanks to what we know about our personal life cycles, we know there's a good chance we personally won't be around long enough to reap any of this promised future richness (jam tomorrow). And second, no one is precisely clear about how the osmotic process actually works. All they know is it takes some gurus, some books and some ordinary managers like us to read them and do something different as a result.

So there you have it in pretty crude (and cryptic) definitional terms: we live in a business world where everyone is an expert and where everyone and everything is desperately scrambling for a finger-hold on the great life cycle and making sure that if anybody falls off, it's going to be the other guy.

In this changing and uncertain world, no matter who's left standing when the music stops or who slides away out of sight when the cycle shifts, we can all be sure of one thing: the gurus and the conventional wisdom will still be around to proclaim the exact why and wherefore of it all, and to spin the cycle round again. That's a measure of their power.

Admittedly that is perhaps too cynical a view, but nevertheless it is hard to know what we can trust in an environment like this where we all have pressing things to do, deliverables and deadlines to hit. In fact it is hard to see where trust fits in at all, or what its role is or even what the word means. That's where this book comes in.

Value Propositions

Business is about money. We make the case that it is also about trust – about managing the risk of consciously behaving in ways that benefit others – our working definition we developed in the opening pages.

We do not directly make the claim that more trust equals more money (although that is clearly the case, as we will show later). More crucially, the message is that, in the environment we have just described, moneymaking opportunities are severely constrained without trust.

In fact, without trust everything is severely constrained, everything underperforms. In guruic terms this comes out as 'all systems tend to sub-optimize'. The message is simple: if you trust, you benefit. And if you don't, you don't. This is the case whether you are a firm or an individual.

Whatever it is, business is business, and it takes place wherever and whenever an opportunity presents itself. It always has and, so we must hope, it always will. This will be the case whether the reader chooses to stick with this book or not, of course, but it is maybe worth bearing in mind that the authors are risk managers who understand business risk as well as the pointless impossibility of trying to manage business risk without first actually taking that risk.

Trust is a gigantic topic with connections everywhere. This has led us to build a book that is a bit like a swimming pool: it has a shallow end (which we're in now) and a deep end. We have aimed at keeping the shallow end deep enough to do this huge topic justice and the deep end shallow enough to reassure you that we are really risk managers who know where we're coming from. (And where we're coming from isn't an ivory tower.)

So that's the deal, that's our value proposition. In return for your time and energy we offer you some insights, some entertainment and some upskilling possibilities that might enhance your grip on the slippery slopes of the life cycle.

How it All Started

The basic requirements for doing business are the same as they have always been and they are not likely to change much: someone with a demand for the benefits provided by some goods or services gets together with someone willing to supply those goods or services for a consideration acceptable to both parties and they do business. In a perfect world you would add up all these transactions, scale them up so that every demand is supplied and every supply consumed, and you'd have yourself the perfect business economy – countless neat and tidy buying and selling decisions and everybody happy. So far so simple.

Today's business world though is anything but simple (or happy, for that matter). It is a densely connected place full of risk from crucial interdependencies that are not always apparent and rarely understood.

Business success in this sophisticated world is measured in many ways – profitability, market growth, market share, earnings per share, brand reputation, talent retention, credit rating – the list is familiar and endless. When times are bad, survival itself – corporate and personal – is deemed a success, often the sole success. As often as not, these success measures are the only means the business has of steering its course into the future.

For whatever reason they do it, and however they measure it, business leaders seek – and achieve – success by the judicious and strategic allocation of scarce resources. And, just as it is with success measures, the list of business resources at their disposal – people, processes, capital, information, capacity – is likewise familiar and endless.

It is also incomplete. Trust is missing. And trust ultimately underpins everything that business depends upon. The limiting factor in business development is no longer the availability of resources but imagination about ways of collaborating.

Some Model Ideas

Sine qua non is a neat bit of Latin. It means *without which nothing*. Trust then is the *sine qua non* of business, its only scarcity arising as a result of it rarely being used. One of the great thinkers of modern life, Marshall McLuhan, would reckon it's a little more serious than simple desuetude though. He would maintain that our capacity to trust has in fact been amputated.

According to McLuhan, technological progress extends us – the telescope extends the eye, the car extends the foot, the phone the ear and so on. And, just as every upside has a downside, every extension comes with an amputation. In what is a devastatingly accurate critique of change, not all of McLuhan's examples are as trite as eyes, feet and ears. We have consequently suffered some fundamental and irretrievable losses. Trust, McLuhan might have argued, is one such loss that the downside of progress has teased from our grasp.

The basic systems model that underpins this book is based on McLuhan's insight. We explore the dynamics by which businesses have become extended into mere moneymakers and make the case that it is precisely this extension that has amputated trust. We look at ways of re-attaching it while at the same time enhancing the moneymaking capabilities.

McLuhan notwithstanding – and his work has lots to contribute to the debate, as we shall see later – trust is in fact abundantly available. The capacity that trust has to enhance the productivity and effectiveness of truly scarce resources represents an untapped seam of boundless wealth waiting to be mined.

In later chapters we define and examine the relationships that enable trust to work. We argue that business success directly reflects the opportunities trust makes possible. By the same token, the absence of success reflects the absence of trust. The impact of trust and the opportunities it makes possible are where business benefits lie. And, for its impact to begin to be felt, trust need be nothing more than a conscious undertaking by a business to behave in ways that benefit others. Critically, a business gets trust by giving trust. And if it doesn't, it doesn't.

To Trust or Not to Trust?

To trust or not to trust – to adopt behaviour in line with our working definition – that is the question.

Trust is not a judgement about trustworthiness, it is entirely an act of choice and we all make choices all the time. In fact many of us are paid expressly to make choices. So what's the problem? Why do we typically choose not to trust?

Trust begins with the notion of choice itself. Choice, in business, generally implies making a selection from a set of options. This means even having tea at the Ritz we're constrained by what's on the menu. If trust is not on offer how can we choose it?

In reality the choices we allow ourselves to have come about as a result of the way we construe our situation, on how we feel about things, on the context we find ourselves in and on the possible implications of the choice we're about to make. And that's where the problems start even before trust is involved.

Immediate Concerns Are Pressing Needs

All of us carry around with us a set of immediate concerns – pressing and real issues that dominate our existence and that constrain the choices we allow ourselves. We use them as defence mechanisms, we use them to justify irrational choices and we use them to delay the decision-making point as long as we feel we need to. If we let them, immediate concerns can take us over entirely. Everything else is excluded. The implications for trust when we are in such a state leave us open to all kinds of manipulation. In ancient Florence the infamous Niccolo Machiavelli made a name for himself by exploiting the power of immediate concerns. He perfected a way of getting all manner of legislation on to the books while the citizens' eyes were elsewhere, usually focused on immediate concerns he himself had created. Over the centuries, it is safe to say, we have all been his victims one way or another.

It is somewhere written that the love of money is one of humankind's more unappealing immediate concerns from which all manner of nasty and Machiavellian things flow. Despite this, at some level we invariably – some would say inevitably – choose to let money be our dominant immediate concern.

If you had asked a wise man, back in the days when there were such things, the difference between a rich man and a poor man, the chances are he would have said something to the effect that they act differently. Ask a poor man, in any age, and he'll say money.

Whatever the biblical case against loving it, money itself has a long and not altogether distinguished history. It also serves a multiplicity of functions almost all of which impinge on our immediate concerns one way or another. For this reason alone, money's role in trust can never be overlooked nor underestimated. Trust though we take to be deeper rooted than money.

For the parties involved, the barter transactions that predated money were rarely entirely equitable. As such, participants rarely felt able to trust such transactions although they ran on trust. The coincidence of mutually acceptable wants that could be satisfied by exchanging lumps and bundles of goods and services almost never came about. That's probably why poets starved in garrets – how many loaves of bread is an ode worth in a barter economy? Who would trust herself to write a poem in such a place?

Money, by enabling trust, introduced a new basis for choice. It extended us, McLuhan would claim, amputating our capacity for barter relationships in the process. Not only that, with money, economic man was born, for whom more is always better. And with economic man came the gloomy science of economics. This rapidly shifted immediate concerns away from the direct benefit of the commodity to the opportunity benefit of money itself. Or, as market-eers would have it, from the sausage to the sizzle.

Despite the great leap forward money made possible, money-based transactions are nonetheless still rooted in a barter arrangement as inequitable as any. This is the 'value for money' barter that stems from the fact that we are all economic man. The result is that we trust not the person we are transacting with, but rather that person's behaviour in being predictably greedy. In doing so we keep the economic wheels turning but miss the potential in the other person's behaviour.

In the event, then, any choice we make inevitably reflects our immediate concerns. Everything else is driven out of our heads. The flavour-of-the-month success measures we have already looked at – working capital turn, headcount, cash flow, gross billings etc. – frequently translate into a firm's immediate concerns and as a consequence underpin every decision. Hence the simple guruic wisdom that you get what you measure.

Survival is a pretty powerful driver in the context of immediate concerns – the fear of not having a job or of being wiped out by the competition is a good way of getting attention and keeping focus. So is toothache. So, in its own way, is where to spend next year's vacation. Whatever they are, immediate concerns, by their nature, invariably leave little or no space for useful trust. There's only one choice on the menu of a guy with raging toothache.

So to trust or not to trust is a choice we have to make in the face of our limitations. And although it is arguably a mere truism to say we are limited by our limitations, it is true nevertheless. Skill-set limitations, for example, unarguably confine a person's primary engagement with the world – work opportunities – to a narrow area.

The same goes for trust. Its absence – its omission from the menu of available offerings – confines a firm's primary engagement with the business world to a narrow and narrowing area. The reasons for this lie in the nature of business itself.

The Nature of Business

Trading, as we have seen, stopped being merely person-to-person transactions when money replaced barter as the primary business driver. Relationships as a result started taking on the character of the things – the commodities – that were being traded. These quickly acquired a rationality and autonomy of their own – a 'phantom objectivity', it has been called. Soon they totally displaced the person-to-person relationships that had driven the pre-money economy.

Soon also, a person's labour became undifferentiated from the product of the labour. Soon the person became alienated from the mechanisms of the economy. Karl Marx called the process reification.

In the context of trust, reification is the process we use when we take something that is abstract and create an imaginary picture of it as being real, concrete even, and with human characteristics. Uncle Sam and John Bull are reifications (not only that, they are reifications in which we are conditioned to have trust). We also use reification to turn real people into machine-like or thing-like things. So people become 'MBAs', just as they become complaints, interruptions and window cleaners.

Reifying things helps us fit them into the mental picture we have of the world. As a way of getting a handle on abstractions of all kinds, reification is immensely powerful. So much so that it permeates our entire culture. Stereotyping is a particularly pernicious facet of reification – think of an 'Oxbridge type' or an 'estate agent'.

We all reify all the time and although Marx first identified it as a business phenomenon of change, he did not invent it. In fact, Søren Kierkegaard, the profoundly religious inventor of existentialism, wrestling with his own personal 'phantom objectivity', probably best summed up the power of reification when he said 'God doesn't exist, but He is real'.

Now, here's a bit of reification: reification is not essentially a 'bad' thing. There are huge risks associated with it though – particularly as far as trust is concerned. In the great way that he had of presenting the world to us, Marshall McLuhan took the power of reification to its ultimate in his famous maxim 'the medium is the message'. This, as we will see below, is never more true than when it comes to trust.

Trust, then, is what will enable you to look at a building site and see that the person operating the JCB is different from the work the JCB is doing. Trust quite simply restores humanity.

Trust is also what enables you to see beyond brand image – self-reification – of competitors, business partners and, crucially, yourself or your own firm. In other words, trust is a real-world value enabler and naturally the 'real world' is a highly reified place. So much so that we're encouraged to think of it as having a mind of its own.

Philosophically it probably does have. For example, we all have some kind of picture of 'western democracy' and 'the business world' and 'Hollywood' – a picture that helps predict what it would be like to go there and how it would react to certain events. That's real-world reification today.

Lots of great thinkers have been engaged in mapping the world's mind and trying to predict its thought waves since time itself began. And they're still at it, thank goodness.

Overcoming Limitations

One of these is Professor Albert Borgmann, who describes one of the ways the world has used to overcome its limitations and help us to enjoy richer lives with minimum hassle. He calls it the device paradigm – a powerful and informative way of looking at the world and our immediate concerns.

The device paradigm comes about with the shift from 'thing' to 'commodity'. In Borgmann's world a horse, for example, is a 'thing' and – let's be frank – a horse is pretty much a 'thing' in anyone's world.

It's the 'thing' that's the thing with Borgmann though, not the horse itself. In this context a 'thing' involves toil if it is to enrich our lives – rather like working for an MBA does or reading a book like this. A horse, for example, needs stabling, feeding, grooming and exercising, it needs taking expensive care of when it's unwell and so on. Around the horse 'thing' a whole social infrastructure evolves in which all the players fully understand their roles and responsibilities and whose place in the hierarchy is determined – limited – by their skills. Status in this world attaches to the job. The job in turn reflects skills and capabilities. So the groom lords it over the stable boy and the jockey over the groom. Oh, and as a result of this 'thing' someone or something gets transported from A to B. And maybe back again too.

That's the world as it used to be under its old reification – a place full of 'things' on which social order was built. A place in which, in our little example, the transport 'ends' were inseparable from, and inextricably tied into, the 'horsey' means. Then along came technology.

Technology's aim – OK, I'm reifying technology here too: it doesn't really have an aim – is to commodify the stuff we used to get from 'things', to detach ends from means. So today 'transport' is largely a commodity, the ends of which, thanks to technology, we can enjoy and exploit to our hearts' content, unencumbered by the means taken to deliver it to us. And without the hassle of maintaining 'things'.

(Horses are still 'things' of course in every sense and still a burden to operate and still support a hierarchy of social standing, but the reward of keeping them – horsey ends from horsey means – is no longer merely the mundane utility of transport referred to above. Horses have moved into the reified world of choice that reified technology has made available to those able to afford it.)

And so 'things' give way to 'devices' in this brave new world. And, thanks to technology, devices have machinery that, unlike a horse, makes no demands on our skills, strength or attention. McLuhan would reckon our skills of horsemanship have been amputated. Borgmann suggests devices simply unencumber us. The same goes for the laptop on which this deathless prose is being written. McLuhan would (rightly) claim that my ability to work the mainframe on which I very first typed has been amputated whereas Borgmann would maintain I've simply been unencumbered from the need to do so. Everywhere in our lives, devices deliver us on-demand commodities and, as a result, we all get, if not something for nothing, then more for less. And economic man is satiated for a while.

Satiating economic man is one thing. For the model to do real work, however, it has to deal with the world as it is. This means it has to deal with POSIWID and the medium being the message.

POSIWID: The Purpose of a System Is What it Does

From cybernetics, and from the insights of quality pioneers such as W. Edwards Deming, comes the simple but profound understanding that a system is what a system does. Its purpose can be read from its behaviour, and is not really a matter of proclamation or protestation at all. If a division of a business consumes lots of resource and produces no significant product then that is what its purpose is. If the National Health Service is a battleground for political power between administrative managers and doctors and consultants then that is its purpose.

POSIWID generally is not understood by reformers and change agents. When a system is 'changed', 'reorganized', 'rationalized' or 'refocused', its purpose is still what it does.

POSIWID: The Model, the Natural World and the Business World

There is a symbiosis between the system as environment and the people who make up the system that stabilizes behaviour and repairs damage. The conscious and unconscious ways people pay attention to and respond to the nature of their environment go well beyond anything that can be understood, still less designed for.

An ecosystem produces its own environment, one that fully accommodates the life-sustaining needs of the species that live within it. Species and populations may come and go but the ecosystem is always self-sustaining and self-stabilizing.

As a metaphor for business environments we need to recognize that organizations adapt to the full range of management initiatives in rich and wonderful ways. And the organizational systems that result wear their heart on their sleeve: their purpose is what they do.

There are plenty of trust implications in this systems understanding of organizations. Trust is definable as being cooperation with purpose. When someone joins an organization he makes a psychological contract. In return for having certain sorts of security needs met, he will behave in certain ways and respond to instructions from certain people. Jobsworth is the place that this contract pushes people. The organization does what it does, needs resource to do so, employs people to do what the organization does. The patterns and the dances of behaviour that this produces, and produces very reliably and consistently, have been well explored (for instance by Barry Oshry). The trust equation is rather 'lowest common denominator': *I trust you to provide me with job security and you trust me to do what I am told.* This is very bottom left-hand corner of the model behaviour.

A large part of the imposition comes in defining what we call a firm's 'enclosure of cooperation'. When you join Tesco, HSBC, the police, the army, the Roman church, a new relationship, the Athenaeum Club or whatever, you are presented with an enclosure of cooperation. It works this way: in return for security of this level – 'jobsworth' membership benefits – your public persona/demeanour is to be this, your place in the hierarchy is this and your freedom of choice is A, B or C.

By implication, 'trust-free' job design increases sub-optimization. This lets us see the Enron–Andersen relationship as being the coming together of separate enclosures of cooperation that are largely discrete, the overlap being the 'consultancy' arm of the auditors. This is a classic Chinese Walls trust marker. Note also Groucho Marx and his misgivings about belonging to a club that would have him as a member.

This is of course not the end of the story, because of our ability to be reflexive and ask whether this is what we want. If we do not want the NHS to be about warring administrators and doctors, even if we ourselves are administrators or doctors, then we can discover what we really want the system to do and it will change of its own accord. To do so we need to trust ourselves to know our own hearts and minds and we have to trust those around us not to construe reflection and openness as weakness.

In the final chapter of this book we deal with the notion of balancing risks. In the business world any organization we join can fail and thus betray our trust in it. Once we acknowledge that an organization is no more or less than its members and their relationships, then we can start to understand how our psychological contract with it affects not just our individual risk of being rejected by the organization but the joint risk of the organization failing. In this sense, small and risky organizations are healthier than large and ancient organizations, because it is easier for members of the organization to make this step.

The preference is for people to be in some way plonked down in the required place within the organization's trust space and not to move. The notion that managers should take responsibility for the organization having an appropriate purpose is deeply damaging from this perspective, and leads to a succession of poorly founded initiatives that taken together push the organization towards a 'jobsworth' culture.

By conducting a proper analysis of trust we see the engine room of organizational behaviour and organizational performance. It is the trust equations that determine the underlying purpose that will out in seeing what the system actually does. The elements of organizational design and development have these equations as an inescapable foundation. All forms of external motivation and coercion are mediated via that fundamental psychological contract that sets up the deal.

The Medium Is the Message

McLuhan's assertion seems to have had a subliminal effect on practically everything that has been written since he first uttered the words. Whatever its absolute nature, the role it plays in trust and risk management can never be discounted. We have already touched on the world's knee-jerk tendency to shoot the messenger. The mere mention of the words trust and risk, by some strangely less threatening means, focuses attention on usually overlooked aspects of operations. As such, radical choice options become available that otherwise would remain closed. Such is the power of the medium and such is the power of the message.

A Case of Paying Attention to Trust

The police force, with its procedures, powers and presentation, is a living embodiment of the medium being the message. As such it makes a fitting example of the application of the trust model to business performance to close off this introduction.

In trying to create a framework within which their performance can be measured and managed, it is important to understand the stakeholder relationships that allow them to do their job at all. In some high-profile recent cases, such was the level of distrust between the police and the community that they found it impossible, despite a huge input of resources, to mount an effective investigation.

The context of this work is an existing measurement scheme that is widely thought not to represent the reality of 46 different police forces and which shows no significant trends over the past five years.

Table 1 Trust model for the police force

Type of trust	Relationship type	Key properties	Areas of police performance	Key stakeholders
Authority trust	Institutional and centralized command and control	Consistent, single point of failure, bureaucratic	Home Office policy implementation, legal rules about evidence	Home Office CPS Courts
Commodity trust	Consumer service provision, service level agreements	Dominated by (fickle) consumer perceptions, volatile	The beat, public order policing, national stories	Public Press Event organizers
Network trust	Social integration, normal citizenship	Inconsistent, local, community based	Information gathering in the community, recruitment	Communities Social institutions Other agencies
Authentic trust	Individual and personal, leadership	Based on internal values	Respect for citizens, inspiring support and confidence	Citizens Witnesses

Trust has a double importance for a performance measurement framework:

- Police work depends on all the different types of trust. The framework needs to be sensitive to its effect on this enabling trust: we cannot assume that measurement will enhance trust.
- The communication of meaningful information between parties using the framework is also dependent on trust. To the extent that the parties do not trust each other to use the information responsibly, the information and its potential meanings will degrade.

Unless the police can balance the different sorts of trust required for them to be effective, performance in one area will be at the expense of performance in another (Table 1).

PART 1

Authentic Trust Is the Gold Standard

Authentic trust is a personal thing. It is the trust we give to others because that is how we are and that is the choice that we make. It is the only aspect of trust that is not (and cannot be) imposed on us from outside so its influence, leverage and power all work internally on us. It comes from our own sense of self and relationship and is not instrumental, not 'for' anything.

Authenticity represents our ultimate freedom of choice and achievement and, personal as it is, authentic trust nevertheless always implies trusting *someone* or *something*. In doing so we give up a measure of power over ourselves and become open to the influences and leverage that exist in trust's other dimensions, as we shall see.

In the absence of authentic trust our lives become taken over by *publicness*. This is the loss of the authentic self that arises from conformance with imposed preconceptions, options and values. Publicness describes the situation where the choices and the messages are dominated by the expectations of the people those choices are visible to.

Authentic trust runs from zero, where complete publicness is the required price, to full trust, where that trust flows from a person's authentic choice. Transparency and accountability often preclude trust by promoting publicness. In our model there is increasing concern for public face to the left and increasing concern for personal

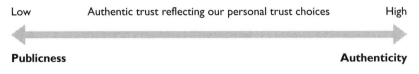

Figure P1.1

integrity to the right, the dimension in the model is as shown in Figure P1.1.

Authentic trust holds the core meaning of trust: when we understand what authentic trust is then we can begin to understand the other types of trust. So we start with the gold standard and then move to other meanings of the word which are important in the business world but which are misleading if we take them as fundamental or archetypal. For example, branding and advertising as we know and love them and which we shall see depend on combinations of commodity trust, network trust and authority trust, would be impossible without the existence of some understood level of authentic trust.

At first blush authentic trust is so different to the other types of trust that it might be a topic on its own. In authentic trust I am making choices myself about my own actions. The choice is about a relationship but it concerns solely my behaviour. When the choice is mine then the risk is also mine. Since it concerns me before it concerns anyone else, the choice to trust is a choice I can always make, although the conditions for it being a productive choice are sometimes sorely lacking.

In the other sorts of trust, relations are the other way round: either I am asking someone else to make a choice or I myself am being asked to make a choice by someone else. The choice and the impact have been separated. Of course this is the normal case for business cultures – it is almost always about getting other people to do things: customers to buy, suppliers to be more reliable, employees to be more productive, regulators to be less stringent, and so on. Outside authentic trust the possibility exists that the impact of risk can be ameliorated by off-loading it, sharing it or in some way discounting it. That is why the other sorts of trust figure prominently in this book and that is why we must deal with authentic trust first.

Conditions Far from Certainty

Entrepreneurs starting new businesses tend to be hands on. They take the key decisions themselves, they take on personal risk, they only expect others to support them and follow in their wake. They look to change the way some part of their market is understood: entrepreneurial action almost always involves new meanings and reconfigured business relationships. This is one example of operating far from certainty, when much of what is taken for granted by others is held to be ready for reinterpretation.

Notice that in these cases, the people forging the change are leaders and actors, not managers. They change themselves first, they take risks themselves first, and they own the issues in an important way. In this context we can see authentic trust and where it operates fairly easily. Entrepreneurs are not seeking to impose their view of the world on others; they are looking for people who want to engage with the new realities being forged – the innovators and early adoptors of the life cycle.

The history of corporations taking over small entrepreneurial companies is that in the majority of cases the innovation and creativity cease: the corporation cannot respond to the call of change, they want the products but not the process that creates them. The corporation wants the entrepreneur to trust the corporation. And that is a different sort of trust. It is not authentic and it is this distinction we want to emphasize.

If meanings and markets are in a state of flux, then relationships need to be stable to survive. Business is used to the other extreme, where ideas about productivity and profit are thought of as unchanging and people are moved around to maximize this and minimize that. But forging new meanings and getting them adopted widely as a source of business value takes stable and deep relationships between people. Because authentic trust is always between people it tends to both generate lasting relationships and require stability to prosper. Organizational change programmes are likely to damage what trust exists, and indeed they are often designed to disrupt organizational meanings that managers want to change.

Rational and Reasonable Action

Our view is that the majority of business logic is after-the-event justification for choices that were made. It is to do with accounting for actions, not about action *per se*. At its best this can be a case of testing business decisions to see how they hold up against the numbers. At its worst it takes away any notion of authentic action. As Enron and Andersen illustrated so beautifully, it is far easier to try to make the numbers reflect the business's needs than it is to take authentic action to put things right.

So within the space colonized by business people as rational and reasonable, there will be no authentic trust, as there will be no authentic action. These cultures do not allow people to say, 'I am trusting you because that is what I choose to do, and I want you to respond to my trust, which will continue because I continue to choose to trust you'. Such a statement will be attacked by business rivals, who will subvert it and treat it as an exploitable weakness.

But there is another view of what constitutes rational and reasonable action that says that if a business goal can be envisaged that relies on trust and stable cooperation then the competitive and individualist logic that passes for rationality must be treated as a barrier to be overcome. If we, jointly, can have an aim that implies trust, like mountaineers on a Himalayan peak, then there is nothing remotely unreasonable about pursuing it given the insight that it depends on trust.

Parallel Universes

What is separate is also connected (to get into a Zen frame of mind). Our social systems do not work by simple cause and effect, they are too complicated for that. The business culture that says 'we need to do this because we know that it leads to the outcomes we want' is already delusional, but the delusion is safe and self-fulfilling. So the same situation observed by different people with different philosophies will lead to different observations and different interpretations: try it.

The result is that when certain people take the step of authentic trust and see the possibilities flower as people respond to it, others

AUTHENTIC TRUST IS THE GOLD STANDARD 41

will interpret the same events according to ideas of cause and effect in which trust does not play a part. This is inevitable. These are parallel universes where different things are paid attention to: there is no proof, no incontrovertible evidence, no experimentally reproducible effects, just human action.

Trust is not a law of numbers issue either. We cannot make statistical inferences about the effects of this or that trust move. That is reasoning from the other universe, where the consequences are held to motivate the action. We discuss utilitarian thinking – the idea that actions are right because they are useful – later on in the book. So while it is difficult to suspend the habits of a lifetime of normal business culture and reasoning, bear with us. We are simply saying that that reasoning has been proved not to lead to where we want to go.

Introducing the Shadow Side

For every system of self-reinforcing positive attitudes, motivations and actions, there is a corresponding set of negative ones that we call the shadow side. Mistrust is a handy metaphor for labelling the shadow side, although – as much as misplaced trust – it more closely reflects an absence of trust practically amounting to ignorance that trust in any form exists. The shadow side is a system that anyone can get pulled into, and we have more to say about it in the final chapter. For now consider shadow side stakeholding (Figure P1.2). This diagram shows a space with corners occupied by:

- *hubris*: the belief that everything is under control;
- *abdication*: the abandoning of control to others;
- *seduction*: the use of false promises to exert illegitimate control.

From the evocative set of words on the diagram, we want to pay special attention to some symptoms of shadow-side systems that we think are useful diagnostics:

- Task perfection is the belief that the job can be done right irrespective of context, and that doing it right is somehow self-justifying.

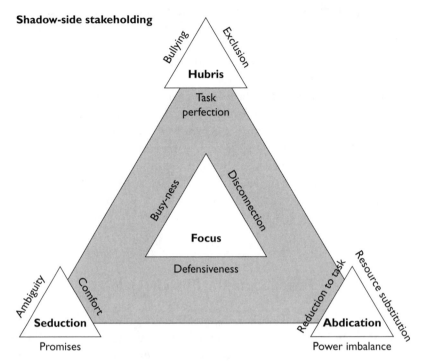

Figure P1.2 Shadow-side focus comes from hubris, seduction and abdication

- Busy-ness is when the whole world is filled with urgent tasks that do not allow any space for different perspectives or for debate about other people's perceptions.
- Resource substitution is the belief that ultimately any task can be done by someone else and that in the end people are inter-changeable resources in getting the job done.

For the purposes of Part 1, authentic trust is a bulwark against these sort of beliefs and this sort of shadow-side system.

1

Authentic Trust

In order for us to trust ourselves to understand and to be understood we first of all have to trust the language we use. So definitions are important.

Some 'hard' business definitions – debtors, creditors, inventory, working capital, share price – can and do contribute unambiguously to understanding. It's not all good news, though, as we will see later. When unambiguous things become the sole focus of business performance metrics, as they frequently do, they as often as not have a sub-optimizing impact on the bigger picture. Worse than that, in becoming ends in themselves, their unintended consequences deny the business any useful space for trust. They restrict degrees of freedom, including the freedom to do better business.

When it comes to defining 'softer' aspects of business there's a different kind of problem though: 'Many things in the world have not been named,' philosopher Susan Sontag has pointed out. 'And many things that have been named, have never been described'.

To some extent, both parts of Sontag's observation are true when it comes to authentic trust. Everyone instinctively knows that trust has to do with feelings or belief about honesty and reliability and that authentic has to do with genuineness and trustworthiness. Defining for understanding and being understood though implies a somewhat more detailed description.

Common usage makes a living language a wonderfully powerful and malleable thing. New words are born, old words are revived, accepted meanings become altered (sometimes subtly, sometimes less so) and nuances get added. The implications for communication and understanding as meanings change are almost always left unconsidered. In the looking-glass world of Tweedledum and Tweedledee, words meant simply what the speaker intended them to mean, no more, no less. Think of what Enron meant by sales, Andersen by audit, Barings by fiduciary due diligence, Railtrack by infrastructure and Marconi by strategy, and it's easy to see that in today's business world things can be pretty much the same as they were in Alice's time. When the second-hand car salesman says, 'Trust me' this is not what we understand by and from his appeal.

Trust unambiguously implies a choice, taken by an individual or an organization, to believe that another individual or organization is considering, and ideally acting in, their best interests. Very often in business we do not even consider trust to be an option, let alone a serious choice. But when we do, trust becomes the basis for useful cooperation and in doing so opens up extensive and rewarding possibilities for the way individuals and organizations function and for the way business is carried out.

Trusting is a challenge. It carries implications. It is often a step into the unknown and it is most definitely not a risk-free choice. Authentic trust simply implies considered choice, a decision to trust taken open-eyed, a decision with ramifications.

That trust will be rewarded in some way is well understood in the business world. The understanding underpins huge and continuous expenditure in advertising, marketing, branding, positioning, image building, product development and pursuit of the holy grail of the 'trust-me' logo.

However, trust is emphatically not about the manipulation of other people's behaviour. There is a deep-seated and inescapable contradiction between trying to manipulate someone and trusting him or her. The appearance of trust when manipulation is intended is as inauthentic as you can get.

Seeing Authentic Trust

One of the situations in which authentic trust shines through is where people need to take a stand against the conventional wisdom. In the following software system development case study we can see this at work.

A project was set up to develop a new motor insurance system for a large corporate insurer. The new system was to handle motorcycle insurance and was needed because the marketing department wanted to differentiate the firm's offering in this market sector. The specification for the system was basically 'what we have now with these business rules added'.

Consultants were asked to come up with an architecture for the new system and oversee its development by in-house development teams. The architecture they came up with pulled the business rules out into a subsystem where they could be explicitly and separately maintained, rather than being embedded in the system code as they were traditionally.

The senior manager in charge of this project walked a presentation of this approach and its advantages around the business to show people at all levels how it would generate control for the business and an ability to respond quickly to competitive moves in the market.

The project started to move into murky water when the need to interface the new system with the underlying database and other common services was tackled. People in charge of these other areas could accept the arguments for architectural change but were not about to agree to the simplifications it made possible in their own areas. The work related to the project grew like topsy.

Like many projects of this type, project management consisted of tracking a structured list of tasks with time allocations against them. Despite the huge amount of task work being generated, it was put into the project plan and resources found to do the tasks. The project plan said that the project was within two weeks of delivering, and the huge and boisterous project meetings chaired by the project manager were committed to these time scales.

Between the consultants and the senior manager, enough trust still existed to look at the project from outside the hierarchical trust of the social and technical systems that everyone else was taking their bearings from. An audit was commissioned from one of the big five management consultants who praised the project to the skies but said that it would not deliver for another eighteen months.

The aftermath is also a commentary on authentic trust. The project was abandoned in favour of tweaking the old system. The project management system was never looked at to understand how such a gap between formal prediction and actual outcomes could open up. The project manager retired with a nervous breakdown, never to work again. The senior manager was moved sideways out of harm's way.

Authentic trust makes other perspectives available. It allows the immense weight of hierarchical trust or commodity trust to be borne without becoming engulfed and entangled in their imperatives. By removing the constraints of publicness, and shadow-side mistrust, it allows a different, more radical sort of work to be done.

The patterns illustrated above are the classic ones. In any large organization, there is formality of communication. Systems of communication, of allocation of resources, of accounting for the application of resources and countless similar systems are built up to allow the organization to operate. These systems readily become reified into *de facto* definitions of work and value. People make statements like 'I have spent two days on task x and therefore I have generated y pounds worth of value against plan z'.

It takes another sort of work to map that formal statement into a world where such formality is contingent on all sorts of factors that are never made explicit. There is nowhere to stand within the formal system to make these other judgements, to do this other sort of work. To the extent that the formal systems are implicated in the politics and power structure of the organization, so much so that to ask questions is perceived to be political attack, then this work is politically dangerous, as in our insurance illustration.

Rather than rely on the particular integrity or eccentricity of lone whistle-blowers, we want to look at the sort of trust between people and groups that allows questions to be mutually explored, rather than baldly and bluntly stated when all other routes have been exhausted.

The Risk of Authentic Trust

There is an identity, a 'me', a self that comes to trust. And in trust I open myself up to the other person, to their subjectivity, their interests, their immediate concerns. This is the point and the natural result of giving trust, but it puts me at risk. It may well result in change to my identity. The identity I started with becomes something else, something different, in the act of opening up. This is what it means to have possibility, but that possibility cannot be a supermarket choice, a set of options. It is a new path that opens up with its own logic from a real choice that I made, and it changes the 'I' that made it.

When I involve people around me in my projects and activities, far from seeming to open up new possibilities, it often seems to limit what can be done, what can be achieved. There are too many people to consult, too widely divergent perceptions of what needs to be done, too difficult dynamics in the group. It seems that my choice of trust and relationship leads away from the promise of possibility and potential. What started out as an existential risk seems to end up in the doldrums.

When I negotiate with someone about some future work, the notion of my expectations – of them, of myself, of our interaction – is very important. I can voice my expectations in a way that breaches trust by not allowing any room for the other person to contribute. I can withhold my expectations in such a way that the other person feels I am abdicating my role, or that I have a hidden agenda, thus breaching trust in a different direction. I can breach trust by imposing a structure on the relationship that equally closes down space – that would be the aim. So in feeling for trust there is a subtle dance of respect for the other person and myself that allows an adult, peer-to-peer relationship to emerge in the shape that it will. The delicacy of this operation is due precisely to the risk to, and change of, identity outlined above, on both sides of the relationship.

So we can suppose that the problem with stuck relationships and groups is an inability to navigate the change and possibility inherent in the situation. In my hypothetical project, when I engage with those around me it is not in the spirit that I may be changed by doing so; it is a narrower, more goal-oriented relating that puts the goal ahead of the relationship.

If we are in task mode, in goal-oriented mode, in achievement mode, we are looking to work out some issue or challenge from our current, stable identity. It is our current identity that wants to create this particular achievement. To engage with others while we are in this mode is to co-opt them into our goals. This is a perfectly reasonable thing to do – indeed, the only thing to do if we cannot achieve our goals unaided.

It is not the same act, however, as choosing to trust someone, to work with someone. To do this latter is to put the goal up for negotiation as the other person's subjectivity and constraints are brought to bear on the situation. In this different situation we can expect that the authentic goals for the relationship and what we want to achieve together are different from the original goals. In this way I acquire both goals and capabilities that I would otherwise never have imagined even existed.

I cannot have these assets without the step of trust, because without opening myself to the risk of change I will not be able to perceive them. In giving trust I come to understand, for good or evil, more of the world.

If I am to take this personal risk without undue naïveté or blind faith I need some limits, some safety net, some sense of proportion. This safety net comes from some checking, some grounding, and some testing of assumptions, yours and mine. This is subtle because it must not convey a message of mistrust, must not itself be rooted in mistrust.

In conventional business, this checking is a checking of signs, a checking that the other person is 'stable' or predictable. It is a checking for any behaviour that might indicate a need to revise the relationship, to withdraw trust, even if only temporarily. Of course, it is precisely this need for stability that results in stuckness (where else could it go?). You are stuck because I need you to remain the same and vice versa.

Applying Checking Behaviour

Next time you need to rely on someone, take stock of the way you frame the task. Are you assessing the situation or the person? You may have a model that the reliability and trustworthiness of the person is the key to predicting what might happen. You may prefer to check in what circumstances the person would have a conflict of duties or in some circumstances not be able to meet your needs. Our suggestion is that the first model is unnecessarily and counterproductively *ad hominem* and that the second model is far more likely to lead to good outcomes. We know, however, that people are often reluctant to engage with root causes.

The radical alternative is to trust the relationship ahead of the identity of the other person. If the point is to enable change then there is no point in trying to ground trust in signs attached to the identity of the other person. The continuity is not in the identities but in the trust, a highly paradoxical situation.

The archetypes for this thinking are in our most intense relationships – the mother–child bond or a close marriage. In these relationships it is actually our expectation that the stability and unquestioned inclusiveness of the relationship, its entire lack of provisionality or contingency, enable the growth, development and change of the identity of the participants without this ever raising a question of trust.

If we reflect these understandings back into risk management practice we get an insight into the basic advice that *first you must take the risk*. While our stance is that risk is 'out there' and that we must find trustworthy people to work with, we are actually insisting that no other agenda is allowed to impinge on our own. We have the goal, we are going to achieve it with others, they must therefore keep their identities stable while cooperating with our goals. They are stuck, we are stuck and there are no degrees of freedom in addressing the goal. While risk is out there, no one can develop or grow, but meanings can still change.

When we accept, with the hero archetypes of old, that the quest will never be won without that growth and development – that actually the very point of the quest is the inner struggle – then we see just how stultifying this conventional view can be. How constrained we are by publicness. Not until we are prepared to trust the old woman at the side of the road, to take on board her strange message, can we make progress. The goal is not what it seems to be.

In the case of mutual vulnerability as in a mutually dependent value-chain we can see this logic very clearly. Instead of stating exactly the requirements, service levels and contractual clauses that the supplier must meet in order to meet the needs of the client company, the other view is taken. There is no point in having a supplier who does not contribute to the improvement of the global process. Useful improvements are equally likely from either company and both must be open to these. By establishing mutual vulnerability in operations, problems in the supply chain must be paid attention to in real time without a preconception that these belong to the supplier until proved otherwise. The actual requirements of the client company will be adjusted to meet the supplier's insights into the optimum joined-up process.

Look at the risk analysis in this scenario. A client risk analysis would show a vulnerability to the business plans and operational capability of the supplier(s). A standard response to this would be to put in place contingency plans for handling the eventualities that might arise. On the contrary, what is needed is an opportunity/risk analysis that shows potential large value in these risk events in tuning or restructuring processes within the client and across the supply chain. The conventional analysis, by focusing on fixed identities, systematically removes a potential source of value. What is more, it does so in a way that is completely invisible, resting on some assumptions that are unlikely to be challenged.

2

The Authentic Trust Benchmark

In applying authentic trust we need to understand what it looks like as a business pattern. This benchmark tries to pin the pattern down in compact form.

This benchmark describes a process for the development of authentic trust and a set of trust criteria developed from the process. The benchmark can be used to evaluate claims that a product or process supports or develops trust, by scoring against this benchmark.

Using the Benchmark

Authentic trust can only exist between people. The concept is often extrapolated to try to include products or services that we might trust in the sense of relying on their robustness and integrity. To understand these claims it is necessary to expand the system of interest to include the suppliers and maintainers of these products or services.

Trust that exists between two people is the easiest form of trust to understand. Most of the interesting business situations where trust is important involve three or more parties in a system of interest that must be understood as a whole. If two people have established trust within such a system but mistrust a third party then the system as a whole will not exhibit trust properties.

Where parts of the benchmark do not seem relevant or are difficult to apply, this indicates that a restricted meaning of trust is being employed. This is a common situation and is the underlying reason for using the benchmark. Think carefully about whether the restricted meaning for trust is adequate to the needs of *all* the parties concerned.

The Benchmark

The benchmark is organized into three threads and two levels. Each thread is a distinct aspect of authentic trust, which may or may not be developed in the situation being benchmarked. The first level is a diagnostic to determine whether or not the thread is present. The second level is a set of criteria by which to understand how well developed the thread is.

The questions within the level 1 set give a 'yes' or 'no' answer to whether the thread exists.

The level 2 questions are ranked to imply a degree of development, so you should see 'yes' answers until you come to a 'no'.

Thread 1: The Act of Giving Trust

Trust is present when someone gives it to someone else. The act comes from the resources of the person doing the giving and is not conditional in any way. It may be that trust is returned or reciprocal within the system, but this also must be an act of giving and be unconditional. Authentic trust does not rely on other mechanisms, on the validity of assumptions or on other relationships: it is a radical choice in that sense.

Level 1

(1) In the system of interest can you clearly identify who is giving trust to whom and what the scope of that trust is?
(2) Is the person identified as giving trust able to make other choices than trust without penalty?

Level 2
Trust between parties as identified in level 1 implies relationship and relationship development. The act of giving trust may be a mature, sound judgement or it may be blind and foolhardy. Although the act of giving establishes the initial trust, unless there is a process of relationship development inherent in the act, then trust is unlikely to persist.

(1) Do the parties to trust, in the system of interest, all accept that a relationship between them exists?
(2) Do these parties all have an interest in the maintenance and development of that relationship?
(3) Do the parties each have the personal resources to play their role in the development of the relationships?
(4) Do the parties each have the maturity to understand the demands that the relationships may make on them?

Thread 2: Underpinning Performance

The implications and effects of broken trust run far wider than the immediate cause of the break. Where the parties concerned value trust, measures are taken to avoid situations in which trust is unnecessarily put under strain. The person giving trust will test his or her own assumptions about the situation of the other parties so as to understand the pressures on them, and the ways in which they might appear to abuse or betray trust.

Level 1

(1) Does the person giving trust understand the context within which the trusted parties are working?
(2) Does the person giving trust have any intention of making allowances for context or any way of making such an intention good?

Level 2
If the intention of the parties is that trust between them should grow, then they need to take practical steps to support this growth. They

need to make sure as far as they can that the parties they are trusting are in a position to succeed. They need to test the assumptions they have about the situation the other parties are in, so that their expectations of performance are well grounded.

(1) Does the person giving trust understand the assumptions they are making about the context the trusted parties are working in?
(2) Do they have any practical way of testing those assumptions and dealing with the implications of assumptions that turn out to be false?
(3) Is the person giving trust also motivated to improve the conditions for success of the trusted parties?
(4) Do they have a practical way of supporting the achievement of the trusted parties?

Thread 3: Generating Inter-Subjectivity

One of the important results of trusting someone is that you gain a perspective on the world. To trust someone is to take his or her subjective perspective seriously. They can see things that you cannot, and this is a vital aspect of relationship. Openness and trust are very closely linked. Trust thrives on the respect shown for the insights of the people trusted.

Level 1

(1) Does the relationship between the parties include any mechanism for exchanging their perceptions of their mutual context?
(2) Is there in practice any dialogue that might support exploration of the perceptions of the parties?

Level 2
Trust and relationship development lead to enhanced capability. The improved perspective generated by including the insights of trusted others leads to an ability to see new opportunities and to develop shared purpose.

(1) Do the parties in practice respect each other's subjective perceptions and insights?

(2) Are the parties capable of integrating their different perspectives on their context?

(3) Does the dialogue that takes place between the parties include the notion of joint opportunity?

(4) Is there a sense of shared purpose in the development of the context for mutual benefit?

The Threats to Trust Checklist

The potential for trust is established in the 'The Authentic Trust Benchmark'. Trust once proposed or established can be undermined or destroyed from within the trust relationship or from without. Using a simple but realistic model of trust relationships this checklist goes through the places where trust can be threatened.

You can apply this checklist to a particular trust situation or scenario to generate a context-specific risk log with appropriate risk ownership and responses.

This document is, in a way, a generic or template risk log. We can use a process here of applying the template to a particular trust situation or scenario, and generating a context-specific risk log with appropriate risk ownership and responses. This understanding of context-specific risks is the beginning of managing the risk of authentic trust.

The checklist also provides a basis for classifying proposed mechanisms, including trust products and services. Presumably each mechanism attempts to deal with one or more specific threat. When the risk log is applied to a particular trust situation or scenario, it provides a basis for planning, procuring and implementing appropriate trust mechanisms.

The mechanisms themselves may introduce further risks/threats, and our process here identifies these – or at least provides a basis for paying attention to them.

(1) Undeclared Players
To understand trust relationships it is necessary to establish a system-of-interest with a boundary of some sort.

- Who declares the players – and who might fail to declare some players?

- How do players declare themselves – and who might fail to declare their full position?

The set of relationships that are deemed to be trusting is fundamental to any assessment. The boundary can either be a working assumption during analysis, or it can be the inter-subjective understanding of the parties concerned.

Analysis is then divided into trust issues within the system of interest and issues from without. It is common for people within the system of interest to extend the trust system to others without informing the rest of the system of interest that they have done so.

Suppose the system of interest is a project team. Each member of the team has their own expertise to contribute and there is vigorous debate to establish a common conception of the project task and the best way forwards. If one team member lacks confidence and is relying on the expertise of another colleague without declaring this to the

Name of threat	Undeclared players.
Nature of threat	People within the system of interest extend the trust system to others without informing the rest of the system of interest that they have done so.
Consequences	The person trusting an undeclared player will be found to be in bad faith.
Detecting problems	Players in the system of interest do not have a common operational view of where the boundaries of trust lie. No obvious way of revising the implied limits of trust should the boundaries change for one of the players.
Dealing with the threat	Pay attention to the subjective concerns and perspective of all players. The undeclared player(s) is there for a reason.

project team, the project is relying on the unaccountable and second-hand input of this undeclared player. This can easily lead to a situation where the weak member is thought to have abused the trust of the team, either because of an internal failure or an external leak.

- Do all players in the system of interest have a common operational view of where the boundaries of trust lie?
- Is there a way of revising the implied limits of trust should the boundaries change for one of the players?

(2) Scope and Gaps
We expect there to be a separation in people's lives between different types of concern and in general between their public and private lives. In practice we develop trust relationships with the parts of someone's life that we interact with, and remain blind to those we do not. This raises an implied trust that people will manage their lives so that these separate concerns can remain separate. Because we may not be aware of the way we separate out aspects of our life, it is easy for there to be gaps between expectations and behaviour.

Name of threat	Scope and gaps.
Nature of threat	People fail to manage their lives so that separate concerns can remain separate.
Consequences	Gaps between expectations and behaviour.
Detecting problems	Inconsistency between the explicit scope and the implied scope of trust between the parties within the system of interest.
Dealing with the threat	The parties should check for gaps between their expectations and the assumptions that others are making about scope.

This seems to entail some kind of architectural alignment. Not only do I expect you to separate your concerns, I expect you to separate them in the same way I do.

- Are the explicit scope and the implied scope of trust consistent between the parties within the system of interest?
- Do the parties check for gaps between their expectations and the assumptions that others are making about scope?

(3) Foresight and Maturity
Being able to maintain trust is to some degree dependent on being able to foresee whether commitments entered into will be able to be kept or renegotiated. This takes a degree of maturity in understanding and predicting other people's reactions to potential scenarios in the future.

Name of threat	Foresight and maturity (lack of).
Nature of threat	People lack an ability to understand the implications of trust and what patterns of relationship and consequence may ensue. They may also not be prepared for the emotional strain that trust can entail.
Consequences	Inability to foresee whether commitments entered into will be able to be kept or renegotiated. Inability to understand and predict other people's reactions to potential scenarios in the future. Losing trust when renegotiating commitments.
Detecting problems	Lack of seriousness or gravity when commitments are made. Inappropriate reactions to the actions of others.
Dealing with the threat	Restrict commitments to those appropriate to the maturity of the parties. Develop the maturity to be able to renegotiate commitments without losing trust.

- Is there a realistic basis for the commitments entered into between the parties?
- Are the parties mature enough to be able to renegotiate commitments without losing trust?

(4) Development and Divergence
Trust enables development and change. We should not expect the parties to maintain stable identities or interests. This development is capable of fuelling trust but also of producing a divergence of interests. Divergence can be handled by renegotiation as above but may appear unreasonable and a betrayal of trust to some parties.

- Is there an expectation by all the parties of development and change in all the parties?
- Is there any mechanism to handle future divergence of interest?

Name of threat	Development and divergence.
Nature of threat	Failure to maintain stable identities or interests.
Consequences	This development is capable of fuelling trust but also of producing a divergence of interests. Divergence can be handled by renegotiation as above but may appear unreasonable and a betrayal of trust to some parties.
Detecting problems	Fixed beliefs about relationships. A consistent or persistent lack of exploration of what is changing.
Dealing with the threat	Create an expectation by all the parties of development and change in all the parties. Establish a mechanism to handle future divergence of interest.

(5) Motivation and Interest

There are many reasons why motivation and interest may not be what they appear to be or what they are declared to be. It is to be expected that over a period of time, behaviour will reveal aspects of motivation and interest that were not clear before. There may be explicit subterfuge or there may be subconscious motivations.

- Might any of the parties have a strong motivation to hide their true interest and intentions?
- Is there a divergence between stated motivation and actions?

Name of threat	Motivation and interest.
Nature of threat	Motivation and interest may not be what they appear to be or what they are declared to be.
Consequences	Over a period of time, behaviour will reveal aspects of motivation and interest that were not clear before.
Detecting problems	Alertness to: • evidence of subterfuge; • subconscious motivations; • one of the parties having a strong motivation to hide their true interest and intentions; • divergence between stated motivation and actions.
Dealing with the threat	Move early to reposition trust based on the uncovered motivations. Limit the damage to other relationships.

(6) Content and Communication

The substance or content of a trust relationship, what is communicated between the parties, may not be what it appears to be. It may not stem from the stated motivation, as dealt with above. It may have been intercepted and/or changed by someone not part of the system of interest. It may not be interpreted or understood as it was intended to be. Communications seeming to come from one of the parties may be introduced for malicious purposes or accidentally.

- Is a communication what it purports to be in content, timing, sender, recipients and attributions?
- Is the motivation behind a communication what it purports to be?

Name of threat	Content and communication.
Nature of threat	The substance or content of a trust relationship, what is communicated between the parties, may not be what it appears to be. It may not stem from the stated motivation, as dealt with above. It may have been intercepted and/or changed by someone not part of the system of interest. It may not be interpreted or understood as it was intended to be. Communications seeming to come from one of the parties may be introduced for malicious purposes or accidentally.
Consequences	Either internally to the trust relationship or externally, someone is looking to undermine or abuse trust. They may succeed.
Detecting problems	Is a communication what it purports to be in content, timing, sender, recipients and attributions? Is the motivation behind a communication what it purports to be?
Dealing with the threat	Close communication loops wherever possible and reflect back to the originator what has been understood.

(7) Authentication and Identity

A person who plays a role in a trust system may not be who they make themselves out to be. Or they may have been but are now being impersonated. (The situation where the same person behaves differently because their context has changed dramatically is dealt with above.) If two people within a system of interest are both acting fraudulently, then their validation of each other's identity may be

Name of threat	Authentication and identity (impersonation and repudiation).
Nature of threat	A person who plays a role in a trust system may not be who they make themselves out to be.
	Or they may have been but are now being impersonated. (The situation where the same person behaves differently because their context has changed dramatically is dealt with above.)
Consequences	If two people within a system of interest are both acting fraudulently, then their validation of each other's identity may be worthless.
	Changes outside the system of interest may affect identity – someone's roles and responsibilities in a company might be changed, for instance.
Detecting problems	Are the people within the system of interest who they say they are?
	Are the people within the system still in the same relationship to significant other systems that they were when commitments were entered into?
Dealing with the threat	Make sure that identity and authentication of that identity is not static and based in the past – it is a live issue.

worthless. Changes outside the system of interest may affect identity – someone's roles and responsibilities in a company might be changed, for instance.

- Are the people within the system of interest who they say they are?
- Are the people within the system still in the same relationship to significant other systems that they were when commitments were entered into?

(8) Abuse and betrayal

As well as all the subtle and sometimes unintentional threats to trust, there is straightforward abuse of trust and betrayal, which may or may

Name of threat	Abuse and betrayal.
Nature of threat	Straightforward abuse of trust and betrayal, which may or may not be premeditated. (Note: this does not include the Iago scenario, where someone sets out to undermine or destroy trust between other people.)
Consequences	Trust with the abuser is destroyed. Trust in the larger system will be damaged unless the source of the abuse is dealt with.
Detecting problems	Does anyone within the system of interest (or outside) have a reason to want to destroy trust? Is anyone's mental state such that they may want to tear things down?
Dealing with the threat	Find alternatives for the person tempted or driven to abuse trust. Once abuse or betrayal has taken place, deal with its implications quickly and openly.

not be premeditated. Part of this question is dealt with under changes of motivation.

- Does anyone within the system of interest have a reason to want to destroy trust?
- Is anyone's mental state such that they may want to tear things down?

3

The Application of Authentic Trust

In a situation where there appear to be no options left open, nothing to play for, no life or energy, it is almost certain that people's inclination to trust is being abused. These, of course, are precisely those situations when revolution is in the air, when any alternative is welcome and where radical rejection of the current structures can flourish.

When powerful people say that more trust is needed, they almost certainly, by way of an invocation of the need for publicness, mean that *others* should trust *them* more. What is needed of course is quite the reverse – that they themselves should be more trusting. But that step of opening up a repressive situation is genuinely fraught. People's inclination may not be to reciprocate trust when repression is relaxed. Trust is not a social glue or balm; it is very specific in its context and its referents.

The case of the moaning developers

Working with a software development shop in the subsidiary of a large insurer, we found a constant grumble of cynical attitudes and complaints. Everything the management team did was found fault with. But none of these complaints was ever concrete enough to be decisively and visibly dealt with.

We decided to test the situation by setting up workshops for the developers to take responsibility and control for their own area and to put their ideas and requests to the management team. The developers engaged readily with the task and at some point needed to clarify some aspects of management policy as part of their discussions. Rather than treat these issues as hypothetical we invited the manager into the meeting for five minutes to clear up the points. When the manager left the meeting again the key questions had not been put to him, and the developers had to confront their own responsibility for that.

There was, however, an interesting sequitur. The developers were being trained to deliver a new architecture using new technology on the advice of consultants from head office. When it came to the point of using these new skills the investment case was rejected by senior management at head office in favour of a cheaper solution using the old technology. It seems that the developers knew how the land lay around issues where they were not allowed to have a voice.

The way to develop trust analysis into a programme of action is to understand who needs to trust whom about what. Instead of going to a contractual and sanction-laden place of client imperatives and supplier submission, we need to look at the best-case scenario of what work would look like if everyone cooperated well. What conversations would have to take place for the capabilities of the broader value chain to be fully brought to bear on the job?

Once we understand where imagination and innovation can be brought to bear on the work, then we can understand who needs to trust whom. We can also understand the sorts of checks and balances that people would feel supported by rather than undermined by. We are looking to free people to revel in doing a good job. Once this is the aim then people are able to come forward with insight into what makes it difficult for them to do their job well, at the same time focusing on the spirit of making it easier to trust others and, in turn, release their performance.

The case of the moaning developers above shows how difficult this can be. We are part of highly interdependent networks where there are always people who want to call the shots, sure that their own control moves are for the good of all. We seem to move seamlessly from this insight into the business world to a model that says that only lowest common denominator approaches work. We are forced to prove that any management approach that we use is cost-effective against a narrow set of measures.

To use an authentic trust approach we do precisely the opposite. We say that we should understand how we mutually provide the maximum degrees of freedom for people to do their work well by their own lights. We look straightforwardly at the places where trust is abused and work to understand why and to find a balance where the level of abuse is tolerable and manageable. We only back off from the place of full trust to the extent that we fail to create the conditions for it. Is a measure useful to open up space for people to do a good job? No? Well get rid of it then – what is it for?

This is how high-performance teams work of course. They never dream of questioning the competence of their members while being alive to the importance of catching mistakes and poor thinking in particular cases. To build from the team case to the value chain case is to take a huge step in practical difficulty but not to change the principles or the approach. High-performance value chain teams do exist, and exist because people have invested in finding the right partners and building a relationship over months and years that can sustain the trust.

Sharks and Conmen

Because we live in a connected world and in our particularly poisonous business culture, as soon as it becomes known that trust is available, people will move in quite deliberately to exploit and abuse it. No sooner was the notion of partnering available as a better way of contracting than there were companies that specialized in taking their partners to the cleaners. It is this behaviour, of course, that justifies the cynics.

Using the metaphor of terrorism we know the logic of repudiating this. When under attack by political terrorists, civilized societies say that they will not give up their freedoms and the quality of life they bring just because they are subject to attack and that to some extent the freedoms allow the terrorists to operate. We could use the trust analysis developed here to take that argument several steps further. The only thing that truly undermines the sharks is that they are not successful in their businesses. Success is a political concept and we need a practical consensus that rejects those modes of working. Just as most people know how to avoid loan sharks, most people can learn how to avoid the exploiters and the abusers. To do so, however, implies bringing a very different set of values to bear on making and breaking business relationships.

The Case of the Little Big Five

A dotcom company is set up in Kuwait. It has the usual cycle of heavy investment to get it off the ground and in a position to trade. The owner wants to assure himself and his co-investors that this spend is effective and appropriate. He translates this want into asking the local franchise holder of a big-five accounting firm to perform an interim audit.

The local big five (as the world's leading accountancy firms were known in those days) franchise has never audited a dotcom company before. The dotcom has not yet traded. There are no similar businesses in the region. Traditional accounting targets and international accounting standards do not seem to help or even to apply. What, for instance, is the point of measuring return on working capital employed when the company has zero working capital – no inventory, no debtors, no creditors, no work in progress? More pertinently, how do we even begin to put a value on dotcom innovation and intellectual property? And what about technology turn?

The immediate outcome is that the junior accountants tasked with the work turn to the dotcom company's management for advice on how to perform the audit. It would appear that:

- the franchise cannot or will not get advice from the global company;
- the junior accountants cannot or will not get help from their seniors;
- the franchise cannot or will not advise the dotcom owner of the real status of the audit;
- the dotcom owner cannot open up an evaluation of where to get accounting advice from.

> This situation has zero trust for pursuing the stated business of the dotcom owner, although there is no shortage of cynical explanations of the scenario.

If your reaction to the dotcom story is to shake your head and mutter about the state of the world, then read on. There is, of course a serious commercial possibility in this story that would entail a cooperative building of a business opportunity in which:

- the franchise holder gets to know how to perform a new business service;
- the dotcom owner gets to explore the nature of his assets and how they can be accounted for;
- the management of the dotcom get to establish a transparent framework for success.

Turning this possibility into reality depends on the availability of certain sorts of relationship. Since this is Kuwait, that is a very different question for the dotcom to the same situation in, say, Seattle, and different again to how it would present in Rome. The auditors though, are trusted to have a seamless, global expertise and international accounting standards to have universal applicability.

Notice that what might be labelled trust in this story – for instance, the trust of the owner in the powers of the big five – is on the negative side of this equation, tending to suppress possibility. Welcome to the downside of trust.

Putting Our Trust in Devices

In the introduction we looked at Albert Borgmann's notion of the device paradigm that unencumbers us and superficially gives us more for less. Publicness in our model has similar characteristics. The fact that it unencumbers us from trusting is the problem it poses for us. In fact, as the Kuwait dotcom illustration shows, where trust is concerned, it is easy to see practically everything in terms of the device paradigm: TV brings us the news, we do not have to go and see things for ourselves. So TVs are devices and news a commodity. Ernst & Young produce our accounts without us doing anything (except paying their fees of course). So Ernst & Young are devices and accounts commodities.

In this brave new device world, as we saw, reification – putting human characteristics onto inanimate objects and abstract ideas – is the logical step beyond the device paradigm (how else can I claim that publicness has similar characteristics to anything?). Reification itself has become a device that unencumbers us from the need to look too far or too critically into things – particularly things like trust – that might be scary. It is no less a device than TV and Ernst & Young: it gives us a way of getting a superficial understanding of complex stuff that would otherwise be unavailable to us.

At the margin, reification makes knowledge a commodity. What's more, it gives us a way of personalizing our context that aligns directly with our immediate concerns. (Think about how you feel in a telephone queue to your insurance company when your car's been dented. That's reification.)

The business world (where trust has to flourish) is almost entirely a device world. The dynamics of the device begin to come full-circle when we look at businesses themselves as devices. This is where we need to be clear about the price we pay when we put our trust in devices.

Supermarkets, for example, are devices by which we can feed ourselves without reverting to being the hunter-gatherers of fable. Supermarkets are businesses that are devices and as if that wasn't irony enough, the commodities they deliver to us are themselves commodities. (They are things that have been commodified for our convenience and delectation.)

Supermarkets explain why there is a near universal acceptance that the device paradigm is an appropriate basis for examining organizations. They also provide an off-the-shelf metaphor that describes the business world itself. There are two contrasting views of the business world.

One view is like a supermarket. Everything the supermarket sells is there on display – no mystery, no subtlety; what you see is what you get. At worst, you are baffled by why certain things are kept in certain places, and now and then you may need to be pointed in the right direction. All you have to do is choose, and in the bigger picture all you need to do is to shop around to help competition force prices down. You are the customer and the customer is king.

The other view is like a wilderness. You can explore it forever and keep coming upon new wonders. You could never hope to fully understand the complexity of its ecosystems and why things unfold the way they do. You must tread lightly to avoid destroying the very wonder you have gone to see. By accepting the wilderness for what it is, you can become a part of it. You have a bit part in an unfolding drama.

As we said before, what choices we have depend crucially on how we construe our situation. People have a set of immediate concerns that dominate their existence. They need to be heard, they need to pay the mortgage, they need status, they need to be able to pay for their chosen lifestyle. These needs are real and pressing, often to the exclusion of any sense of there being options or choices to be made. The supermarket is, both in reality and in metaphor, both the answer to and the cause of immediate concerns. It is where you purchase what you need and it is the map of what you will need, what you can need.

Behind the supermarket is a supply chain of businesses looking to exploit the immediate concerns of customers. Their interest is in availability, in shelf life, in gloss and promotion, in lifestyle and ambience, in capturing the maximum proportion of customer spend. What these devices hide systematically are agricultural practices, connections to place and people, and engagement with seasonality and glut. This is a general feature of choice and choosing: you cannot choose without excluding other sorts of choice; you cannot have values without hiding other values.

There is choice, as we have already seen, with its paradigmatic consumer choice, and there are degrees of freedom. Degrees of freedom do not appear on menus. They allow life choices that take us down different paths. And the paths have different outcomes.

Sometimes many choices have the same outcome and are not degrees of freedom in any sense. Sometimes there is a more radical freedom to choose direction. It is rare for life choices to be laid out 'supermarket style' as if in a careers fair. Usually our consumer choice has been swallowed by businesses anxious to exploit the way we are dominated by immediate concerns. Of course, everyone would like to make us believe we have infinite choice while systematically excluding the choices that don't suit them. What else would they do?

Now, our wilderness choices have a different character. We only get choice by respecting the wilderness for what it is. We can destroy it but then we have no choice left and the magic is gone. The degrees of freedom we have are to play different roles in the wilderness but always as a partner. We neither exploit nor are exploited. In understanding how not to exploit and destroy, we understand also how we ourselves can be exploited and destroyed, how our degrees of freedom can be removed by the choices that we make.

Relationship Choices

To represent these choices as individual choices that we either take or turn our backs on is to ignore both the pressure of immediate concerns and the nature of groups and organizations. We cannot stand alone in choosing to maintain our degrees of freedom when all around us people are shopping in the supermarket.

Suppose in business terms we are a potential client for a product or service. The nature of the degrees of freedom open to us are:

- to select a supplier;
- to regard the exchange as a transaction or a relationship;
- to use the relationship to explore the original need.

Very often our degrees of freedom are hedged around by policy and precedent. Suppliers must compete on price and functionality. Risk must be exported to the supplier. Negotiation must be used to keep a supplier aware that they can quite easily be replaced.

If we are short of funds to pay for the product or service, or if we are browbeaten by advertising and news management into believing that one supplier is the only real choice, then our immediate concerns have removed our degrees of freedom. We have no room for manoeuvre, or think that we don't.

Even if we want a relationship with a supplier that expands our possibilities, we may not be able to find a supplier who is not already cowed by his own and his clients' immediate concerns. We cannot summon a mature and caring supplier as we would a genie from a bottle.

Shopping choices are about the past. We have *these* rules, we choose by *these* criteria, we know how to manage *these* suppliers. We can just about guarantee that these choices will generate no surprises and that we will remain in control. In voting for the past we say we do not need or want degrees of freedom, and we typically say it as a group, as an organization, from some sense of needing to band together against a difficult world.

Relationship or wilderness choices are about the future. This supplier can potentially open up these new areas and insights, these new ways of doing business. This partnership feels pregnant with many things we do not even begin to understand. In voting for the future we open degrees of freedom for ourselves and others, and choose potential and possibility ahead of control.

Shopping choices are about the other. Choice is just there for me to select between and if the choices do not inspire then clearly the supermarket is deficient. Wilderness choices are about me and about what I can conjure up. They may be desperately dangerous and uncomfortable but I do not locate dissatisfaction and constraint here as I do with the other.

Needless to say, if we neglect degrees of freedom in making our choices, we end up with no degrees of freedom left, with no choice except choices that do not change our immediate concerns and our sense of being trapped by them.

What all this exposes is a lazy and disconnected style of thinking. We train ourselves not to look at the 'side effects' of what we do and what we choose. We have so far bought into a market model of efficiency and progress that we think it almost our duty to rationally analyse what is best value for ourselves and to discount all the para-meters of social and environmental cost. We deliberately decouple the 'cost' of acquiring a product or service from the consequences of choosing. In doing so we lose a sense of who we are and what wider roles we play.

Borgmann's advice is to regain a sense of our focal concerns. A focal concern, like wilderness, transcends the device paradigm and gives us a sense of connectedness – to others, to the environment, to history. Our proposition in this book is that trust is just such a focal concern. Trust has its own power to generate exactly the sort of things we lose by shopping.

The device paradigm is about technology. The point of technology is to make services available, and to make them available where and when we want them, without effort on our part. Technology doesn't reflect on us, although it is common to hear conversations where technology choices are used as indicators of tribal allegiance. When we apply the device paradigm to systems that are not merely technical but have a social dimension, we move into treating people as technology without even noticing. When we catch a train or transact business at a bank counter we are typically working with a device paradigm.

If we trust a machine we mean merely that it is reliable and robust. To trust in this way is not an act, not a choice. It is passive and we think of it as being based on data. When we use the device paradigm (and it is nearly universal) to understand the meanings of our interaction with wider systems, we are dealing with supermarket choice. The supermarket *is* the device paradigm applied to goods. By abdicating our own degrees of freedom in acting in this way we lose our engagement. We lose our sense of agency, our power to make a difference. We become a statistic in the operation of the market.

Machiavelli's insight into immediate concerns is that they hand over power to whoever will take it. If you are dominated by a set of concerns that you think give you little room for manoeuvre, then your behaviour is predictable. It follows that I can manipulate you easily by manipulating your immediate concerns and the forces they apply to you. The business world we know is dominated by a set of immediate concerns that are generated by the actions of businesses on each other. The rising levels of stress and the falling levels of control over business outcomes speak to a system where businesses exploit the immediate concerns of each other and so tighten the noose.

So, logically, there are many degrees of freedom available to the business that can step out of the device paradigm and work directly with people and businesses they have chosen to trust.

Principled Talk and Engagement

There is one immediate implication of the choice to trust or not to trust. If I choose to trust you then the talk we exchange is based in our shared understanding of what we need to do together. One way to think about trust is to think of the space that it opens up for this talk. In trusting you I take on your subjective perception of the world and our situation, thus extending what it is possible for me to perceive for myself. In taking on your perception I also take on your special-ness and your history that has led you to your perceptions: you are a unique individual, not a human resource.

If I choose not to trust you, then talk has to be anchored some-where else. It gets anchored in 'principles', abstract elements of the situation that we share in the culture or – thanks to publicness – pretend to share in order to have talk at all. These principles might be management policies from higher up, theories about how the world works, reported news, whatever, but they cannot be an authentic, engaged perception of the shared situation precisely because the situation is not shared. There is an imposition across the relation-ship of the reality that will get dealt with.

So if I refuse your subjectivity, I have to supply all the necessary perception of the situation. This reduces both what I can 'see' in the situation and my scope for action because everything I need you to do requires convincing you of my reality. Further, you now have a privileged access to my view of the world which allows you to subvert my wishes with impunity. This is the mechanism by which my degrees of freedom are lost.

In anchoring talk in abstract principles, the importance of the principles gets inflated. This is the root of talk about the informa-tion age. It has to be assumed that objective information, relatively free of the need for context, exists and is communicable. In the absence of a real intersubjectivity, which has been refused, we are asked to believe in information that allows us to coordinate our joint work.

This effect also explains the incessant demand for management theory and training, for new approaches that get round the manifest failure of the last fashion. From the perspective of trust, all these theories are broken because they refuse to believe that people perceive very different things and that these perceptions are important to all.

In the introduction we talked of cordial hypocrisy where people claim that organizations are open and welcoming of diversity and difference while acting from precisely the opposite premise, that everyone must sing from the same hymn sheet. Cordial hypocrisy is what fills the gap when principled talk and engagement are missing.

The Creation of Vulnerability

There used to be a controversy between process and praxis. A process is deemed to work in a mechanical way with a straightforward connection between cause and effect. Processes can be tuned or improved in a straightforward manner to increase their useful outputs. This is the legacy of scientific management, given a recent excursion in the form of Business Process Reengineering.

A praxis, by contrast, has at its heart a description of what people do and what they bring to the situation in terms of intellect, trust, perception or whatever. Here there is no straightforward cause and effect link because the people cannot avoid making their own choices about the significance for them of any proposed change in the praxis. The praxis cannot be changed without changing people's relationship with the praxis and its outputs. The only reliable route to improvement is to let the people on whom the praxis rests make their own improvements by their own values and motivations.

In some of the now legendary Japanese manufacturing supply chains, a technique is used to deliberately create mutual vulnerability between partners – the geopolitical equivalent of mutual assured destruction. If one partner has, *de facto*, much more power than the other, then process improvements will be biased to solutions that suit the more powerful player. This will happen both because of force and because of deference.

From a perspective of trust, the imbalance of power removes the reality of choice. I cannot choose to trust the more powerful player because I am forced to accept his actions. I cannot choose to trust the weaker player because in practice if he makes mistakes I will just switch suppliers. It just doesn't matter enough to either of us.

The key Japanese insight is long-term attention to detail and to pursuing consistent goals. So rather than jettison this issue as unimportant, the issue is systematically made more important until the process issues it hides will get addressed. The power imbalance hides process issues of competitive significance in the long term, so the power must be rebalanced by making each partner vulnerable to the other. In a just-in-time manufacturing system this is not too difficult.

By focusing on the need to engage the people directly involved in finding workable process improvements, the conclusion is reached that power stands in the way of trust. In effect, this says that trust is fundamental to improvement and that even apparent advantages of power must be sacrificed to gain the real, wider power to compete.

There is a general principle here that almost all management techniques tend to obscure the very perceptions and information needed to achieve management goals. We can speculate that there is a concept of lean management, one that avoids management interventions wherever possible, one that keeps the reins as light and unobtrusive as possible.

We can think of trust as lean management. All the checks and balances we build into our management systems add no value whatsoever to the management product – effective organization. All the measures, targets, objectives, appraisals, performance management systems, add no direct value – they are props to use while we are learning to work together. We notice that for many people these props become reified – become things in and of themselves. They become the point of management and not a crutch to be cast aside as soon as possible.

Trust is the opposite approach. If I trust someone to do something, to take care of something, I need to nurture the trust but I don't need to measure the output. What would I do with the measure? The point of measures is to help to learn to work effectively together, to have an intersubjective idea of how much we are supporting each other in our joint goals. The moment measures are used as an instrument of control, however innocently or naïvely, they undermine the trust and therefore they undermine the work.

Sometimes systems are so bad – long histories of exploitation, low morale, poorly educated staff, punishing commercial environment etc. – that a harsh regime of targets, discipline, close supervision and mechanical training is the only short-term way forward. Here we want to insist that distrust and dehumanization do not lead to trust and growth in productivity. They cannot lead to systematic process improvement.

Pretending to Be Trustworthy

One major reason why people do not choose to trust is because they do not want to be duped. Confidence tricksters of all sorts know how to find trusting people and know how to exploit their trust for their own ends. This leads to a situation where to be taken in by a trickster is seen to be culpable and shameful.

Our model of trust is not naïve, it is a business choice that is backed by checks on the way the other person responds to trust. There is a huge area of study in the modelling of the incentives the other person might have to appear trustworthy, to mimic the signs of trust while all the time planning abuse(s) of that trust. Part of checking is to understand those incentives and the cost of mimicking the signs that we use to read the situation and the other person. Think of the classic gangster sting operations where hugely elaborate apparent realities were constructed just to trick the target into trusting something they should not.

We extend, give, our trust because we choose to. We know that this is one of very few ways of keeping our degrees of freedom and counteracting a tendency to become dominated by our immediate concerns. If we choose to trust we also know that to support trust in the medium term, we must avoid situations where the reasons to abuse trust become too strong. We need to understand the effect of our trust on the other person and his or her motivations. We need to avoid making assumptions about the other person's behaviour but to be imaginative in understanding the situations that might exist.

PART 2

Network Trust

No man is an island.
John Donne, English poet and
adventurer, 1572–1631

I could never belong to a club that would have
me as a member.
Groucho Marx, trust guru

Whether business organizations or individuals, we all need the sense
of belonging we get from being part of a group. Groups provide
us with security and comfort, and while our needs for these might
differ wildly, membership is nevertheless vital. The power that
network trust has over our lives and business transactions results from
the security and comfort needs we have as individuals and groups.
The higher our needs, the more willing we are to go along with the
group – the more we allow the group's values to be imposed on us
or the more we derive our values from those of the group. The lower
our needs, the more our values reflect our more personally based aspi-
rations and the less willing we are to be swayed by the collective
view. The higher the network trust, the higher the leverage that leads
to (among many other things) the phenomenon known as golden
handcuffs and the debilitating jobsworth culture. To an extent, its
leverage is based on conformity and explains why radical thinking

and independence, by their potential for countering leverage, are often seen as threatening in a business context.

> I stood among them, with them but not of them, in a shroud
> of thoughts which were not their thoughts.
>
> Lord Byron, British poet and
> philosopher, 1788–1824

In general terms the influence of network trust is felt in a micro – a personal – context. Breaking out of its micro confines, it transmogrifies into the all-powerful commodity trust we looked at earlier. In close-up, the network trust dimension of our model is as shown in Figure P2.1.

Needs Must

Security and comfort needs vary, of course – not only from individual to individual and from firm to firm but also from context to context. This explains the existence of the countless groups – formal and informal – that exist in the world. It also accounts for us all belonging to more groups than we would ever imagine. Since it changes as our need for it changes, network trust is inconsistent. That is, whenever it is needed, it simply becomes whatever it is needed to be. Despite this, its power and influence always work in the same way, regardless of context and regardless of the nature of the group, its constitution or the headcount and makeup of its membership.

A highly promising and gazelle-like young runner goes to her athletics club after school for an evening's training with her stablemates in the lead-up to an important race meeting. The coach is unavailable but has left a training schedule for them all to follow. When she gets there the athlete finds that, between them, her colleagues have decided to do something different, something a little less challenging than the coach's routine. Reluctantly, she goes along with them. Back home that night she understands she has let herself down. A feeling of desolation overwhelms her until she comes to terms with the risk we

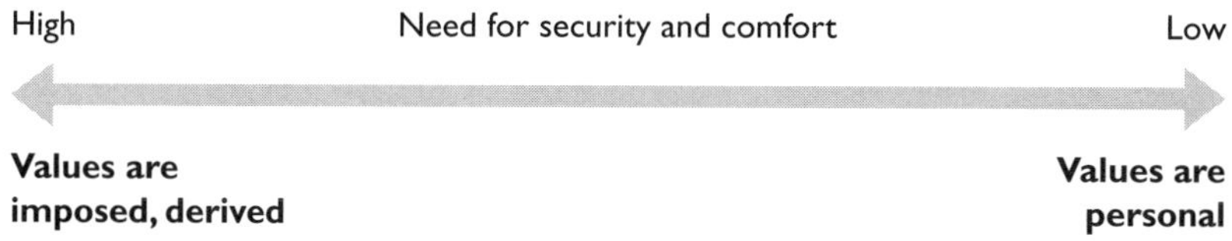

High   Need for security and comfort   Low

**Values are
imposed, derived**

**Values are
personal**

Figure P2.1

all run by being cooperators in network trust. For her comfort and security she took on the values the group imposed. These ultimately proved to be in conflict with her personal choice. In the end authenticity won through and she determined not to let it happen again. She understands that putting her trust in the commodity called training implies giving up certain freedoms and trusting the authority of the coach to make certain choices for her on her behalf. Her desolation certainly won't stop her trusting things in the future (because she's determined to do the best she can in everything she does and trusting is the only way she can do that), although it will teach her something about the risk she runs in doing so and how she can manage that risk for her own benefit.

Dilemma and Tragedy

An illustration of the power of network trust lies at the heart of two of the world's classic case studies – the prisoners' dilemma and the tragedy of the commons.

The Prisoners' Dilemma

The prisoners' dilemma arises in this way. The police suspect two people of having committed a big crime together though they have insufficient evidence to take the case to court and secure a conviction. Rather than see the suspects wriggle out the rap entirely, they arrest them on a minor charge (possession of firearms) for which conviction is a forgone conclusion. The prisoners are kept isolated

from each other and the police separately offer them this deal –
freedom in exchange for evidence that will convict the other one,
who will then face the full sentence (the so-called sucker's payoff). If
they both give evidence in the expectation of going free, they'll both
get let off with a lighter sentence. And if neither of them takes up
the offer (in other words, if they trust one another in cooperating
against the police) then they both just get their knuckles rapped for
the minor offence they are currently charged with.

So (assuming they are in fact guilty) if they both keep quiet they
both gain – big crime, small punishment. If one defects and the other
doesn't the defector gains everything and the other gets the sucker's
payoff. If they both defect they both suffer a lesser punishment.

And there's the dilemma in a nutshell – two choices, three possible
outcomes and no communication within the group. To trust or not
to trust, that is the question. Honour among thieves notwithstanding,
experiments show there is rarely enough trust in place, under any
circumstances, sufficient for a prisoner ever to remain silent.

The Prisoners' Dilemma in Business

One view of the business world sees it as an endless round of prisoners' dilemmas. And in trying to solve old ones we as often as not
find ourselves creating new ones. The dilemmas may not be as clear-
cut or as measurable or as easily turned into a classroom game as that
of the prisoners above but the effect is the same. Look at customers
and suppliers. Look at the relationship firms have with the stock
market. Look at the way analysts react to published accounts. Think
about the contracts we dealt with under commodity trust. Look at
the employer–employee relationship.

Supposing I offer you a job and you take it, then right away we
are both sacrificing something – me, the chance of employing
someone else; you, the chance of alternative employment. I trust you
to be allowed in through the door in the mornings, I maybe trust
you with a budget, maybe with sensitive information, with my reputation, my brand, my clients, and so on. In other words, I trust you
to exercise some power over me. You, in turn, trust me to exercise

power over you. You trust me to pay you, train you, maybe offer you a career path, provide a level of status, provide the proper tools to do the job, take care of the legal niceties surrounding your employment, pay you to take a vacation, and so on.

It is likely to take time for you as a new employee to get up to speed. You may not be fully productive for me for perhaps as much as a year or more. Somewhere along the way, though, I probably have to decide whether you're really what I want in terms of an employee. If you misinterpret my moves in making this assessment you might decide to leave before you actually begin producing for me, taking all your training and new knowledge with you, leaving me with the sucker's payoff. By the same token, I might give you a big project to do and fire you the day you deliver, gaining business benefits on the cheap, so to speak. Or, we could work together to reach a balance of trust and power that suits us both, that satisfies all my employee-trust needs and all your employer-trust needs. Or if necessary I could tie you up in golden handcuffs to keep you on board and your knowledge and power where I can keep an eye on it. And, equally, you could decide that being employed by me is quite simply the most important thing in your life and that you'll do anything (anything at all!) to make sure you keep your job and nothing (nothing at all!) that might expose you to the risk of no longer having it. So network trust is what enables people and organizations to 'use' other people and other organizations.

That the traditional software development process makes for classic prisoners' dilemmas goes without saying given the contractual hoops that have to be jumped through before a line of code gets produced. Since the process generally involves several work groups and many phases, the dilemmas – the network trust dynamics – can become endlessly complex and endlessly iterative. As it does so, so do the contracts.

Quite simply, the client paying for code that doesn't work gets the sucker's payoff. Conversely, the client refusing to pay on account of some technicality for good software means the same happens to the coders. Client and coders working cooperatively – agreed payment made for agreed working code – means both parties benefit, though arguably to a lesser extent than either would have had they been able to successfully defect. Anyone who has ever tried capturing every angle of even that simplified version of events in a contract is sure to feel there has to be a better way of getting the job done.

Costly Irony

Besides being a business minefield attached to a contractual minefield, the software development process is filled with irony, always assuming, that is, that heavy and wasteful layers of unnecessary cost are indeed ironic.

The view that there is an optimum way in which a business process can be carried out and that 'systems' as implemented by businesses generally find ways to sub-optimize the things or processes they are intended to improve, is one that has yet to be shown to be incorrect. So from the outset the software development process is arguably there to deliver systems that sub-optimize. The process itself is sub-optimized and the contractual overlay aimed at countering it, a further sub-optimization.

It needs to be said that software development (and the systems it delivers) is perhaps only the business world's most widely understood, though by no means unique, expression of systemic and costly irony of this kind. It is in fact ubiquitous. Sub-optimized UK public services are a notorious and costly example. The PFI – private finance initiative – payment method is an even costlier sub-optimizer heaped on top of them.

The Tragedy of the Commons

Commons, in this context, are resources that are shared by the group. Access and use rather than ownership are the issues with commons. As well as the grazing ground that is at the heart of this parable, the effects apply equally today to rainforests, carbon dioxide emissions, ozone depletion, fly tipping, traffic jams, and access to and use of many other resources we treat as free goods.

The Tragedy of the Commons

The tragedy of the commons first arose in medieval times. Back then villages had commons on which villagers were free to graze their cattle. Everyone put as many cattle to graze as possible. The more cattle a villager had, the more benefit he was seen to get from the commons.

The more benefit a villager got from the commons the more benefit his neighbours sought. The immediate concern was always to add a marginal grazer and as a result to penalize every other grazer rather than seek out a win–win solution from a shared way of proceeding. In the end too many grazers were added until the commons became unsustainably overgrazed and the land was rendered useless, and both villagers and cattle starved. When the land eventually regenerated itself, enclosed fields began to appear in which only controlled and sustainable grazing was allowed to take place. The commons disappeared and the seeds of modern agri-business were sown.

Today the tragedy of the commons has resulted in the (scarcely believable) proposal for a total ban on fishing in the North Sea as well as entry charges for road vehicles coming into city centres.

The tragedy of the commons is an extreme illustration of the power of network trust. By definition it relates to the group that comprises the entire community. And when the entire community seeks to maximize individual benefit there is inevitably going to be both individual and collective disbenefit. Apart from perhaps air to breathe, few if any universal commons remain in the modern world. Everything else – from water, to security, from education to health provision – has been extensively enclosed and is now delivered by the industry-specific equivalents of agri-business. And even the air we breathe is the same air in which we need to fly as cheaply as possible.

Network Trust Power in Action

The accounting scandals that brought down Enron, Worldcom and the rest and which reduced the Big Five to just four are no less than a tragedy of the commons – the commons that the group of off balance sheet deceivers overgrazed comprised the goodwill and trust of the financial world. Built up over many years, this commons was the basis of the integrity of individual firms and entire industries the world over. At the same time it underpinned the financial security of scores of thousands of people. Network trust, though, as we have

seen, is inherently inconsistent whereas the overgrazing was consistently abusive – demanding consistently increasing numbers with
every report. The commons Andersen destroyed is unlikely ever to
be regenerated to what it formerly was.

Philosophically (and perhaps a little pretentiously and tritely), a
case can easily be made that network trust itself nevertheless remains
a commons. After all, it fits the definition – it is a resource shared
by the group, everyone has access to it, everyone can use it and no
one owns it. What is more, given its inconsistency, it is perpetually
renewable, sustainable and in infinite supply. Trite or not, commons
or not, the fact remains that network trust is an as-yet unexploited
asset for many businesses. The risk of continuing to use commons
that have been overgrazed into diminished utility is escalating costs
being incurred in delivering ever-reducing performance.

In a business context the tragedy of the commons is as sub-
optimizing as the prisoners' dilemma is in software development.
Radical risk strategies demand relationships built on the positive
power of network trust.

Proprietary Software, Genetically Modified
Crops and Groups

Groups come into existence to counter the sub-optimization effects
referred to above. People who share interests come together to
reduce the effect through their collective action. So do firms within
industries or geographic regions. And so do professions. Once the
group becomes a better way of proceeding – that is, once it reduces
the general sub-optimization – it begins to have leverage – there are
benefits of membership and penalties for exclusion – and network
trust comes into play. The group also offers economies of scale and,
crucially, access to the equivalent of its commons.

These commons come in a variety of forms, from pooled information through to joint advertising campaigns, media promotions and
lobbying services. They frequently include industry-specific software,
provision of which solves the prisoners' dilemma and frees individual
members from the development cycle referred to above.

But solving one dilemma, as we have seen, invariably creates
another and the upshot is membership of yet another group that has

power and influence over us. The power in this case is wielded by the most powerful player in the global software industry. Microsoft, of course, is one of the world's hugely powerful brands. It long ago shifted away from being a mere group and today every one of us is exposed to the power of its commodity trust. To an extent we are a universal group. To an extent we are universally sub-optimized and to an extent we are Microsoft's commons.

In a similar way, the USA, the world's sole remaining superpower, is in effect a hyper-power ruling over a group to which we all belong, willingly or not. Its influence is everywhere and is inevitably sub-optimizing. US policy on aid to the developing world for example, differs from the rest of the aid givers. Rather than provide dollars with which supplies can be bought as close as possible to where they are needed (supporting local industries as well as providing aid), the US delivers aid in kind. Increasingly in terms of food aid this implies the delivery of GM crops provided by US firms and developed by US aid dollars.

There is nothing intrinsically wrong with GM food. Millions of us eat it happily and healthily all the time. The problem arises when aid recipients use GM grain as seed corn. In doing so they become commons for the owners of the ruling technology. Exactly like software users.

The point about network trust is the power that it gets from our need for security – and by extension our need to eat and our need to use computers. It is inconsistent, as we have seen – we don't eat all the time and sometimes we switch off our computers. Once it grows too big or too important to live with inconsistency, though, its only way forward is to shift into the realm of commodity trust where consistency is everything (and consequently where the risk of a single point of failure is greater). In explaining the process by which this shift takes place, our model explains how and why the dynamics work – how, for example, by trying to address a little local sub-optimizing dilemma, we risk ending up as commons for a global giant.

4

Network Trust in Action

There are countless little-known facts of business life. The three below are among the least known. And they are killers. Network trust is at the heart of dealing with them.

(1) Risk is often a more significant factor in business success and failure than finance.
(2) Collaborative strategies are the only available basis for understanding and managing risk.
(3) An ability to engage authentic trust provides key insights into collaboration.

Network trust, as we saw in the introduction, is concerned with security and comfort needs as bases for cooperation. As such it has a willingness and mutuality arising from shared immediate concerns that ensure a degree of authenticity is in play. And, just as comfort levels and threats to security vary as immediate concerns change, so it is also inconsistent. The fact that there are infinite network possibilities adds to its inconsistency. Network trust is not only where people 'use' people; it is where the culture of the 'jobsworth' begins.

At its best, network trust works contextually in much the same way as hygiene in Herzberg's motivation theory. That is to say its presence can be a launch-pad towards exercising real choice and exploring degrees of freedom and the radical creation of authentic trust. Its absence implacably closes off these opportunities. (It is probably important at this point to make it clear that 'degrees of freedom' does not imply wonderfully innovative solutions *per se*, although such solutions are of course available. Degrees of freedom merely implies that no possibilities – or impossibilities, come to that – are ruled out, reflecting the energy that network trust has the power to release.)

Because it works in a micro context, its power begins with our personal security needs and those of the groups we find ourselves in. The more we rely on the group for security or for a flow of benefits, the more the power of network trust grows and the more leverage we are exposed to. The more powerful it grows, the more it works to constrain choice, presenting us with fewer and fewer menu options as it does so. When this happens the authentic basis of cooperation becomes compromised and there is an inevitable shift in our relationship dealings towards commodity and authority trust.

The world is as much populated by groups as it is by people – separate groups, stand-alone groups, groups within groups, transnational, multinational and global groups. Just as set theory defines the universal set as the set of everything, we are all, at some remove, members of a global group. That, of course, doesn't stop groups having their own little worlds.

And the worlds of party politics and religion, as well as those of business and the professions, provide endless good examples of the power of network trust in action. For example 'toeing the party line' is vital for any politician aspiring to career advancement. The threat of 'losing the whip' for such ambition spells doom. And ruling cabinets exercise 'collective responsibility' in which the prime minister is merely 'first among equals'. Adherents of religious life may willingly follow strict dietary regimes, strict dress codes, attend regular devotions at prescribed times, make sacrifices unimaginable to the non-religious and acknowledge the infallibility of texts and utterances. Some devotees go so far as joining silent orders, foreswearing all worldly pleasures. The martyrdom defining religious history is an example of network trust taken to its ultimate extreme. Martyrdom in the business world generally lacks the finality of, say, someone stoned to death for their beliefs or burnt at the stake. That said, it is unlikely that the world will ever be confronted with a resurrected Arthur Andersen.

Banking on Network Trust in Action

Towards the end of the last century (sometime in the 1970s in fact) on an early wave of post-industrialism, one of the UK's then five giant high street banks relocated its headquarters to a working-class northern city that had never seen its like before. One way or another, the fall-out from the shift is still being worked through today by both city and bank. Sociology departments in both of the city's universities literally had a field day picking over the ramifications of the move's dynamics.

From a business point of view, one would like to think that if the bank could relive its past or if it decides once again to remove at some time in the future, things would be done a little differently as a result of its thirty-odd years' accumulation of knowledge. The implications for trust, in all its dimensions, have been (and remain) extensive. Here is an illustration.

As Safe as Houses

Just as in every English city around the time of the move, property values and the estate agents' self-serving mantra of location, location, location, figured highly among the immediate concerns of a growing majority of the citizenry. And also, just as in every other English city, the clear property patterns that today allow selection by post-code, had long ago become established and been reinforced through convention and usage. Although it lagged behind some of its richer southern counterparts in terms of house prices, the city had two or three highly select, aspirational districts as good as any in the land. These, prior to the HQ shift, had represented, for most inhabitants, the ultimate rung of the property ladder. The districts' narrow spread of age profiles and lifestyles reflected the market's dynamics at the time.

In trust terms we can say that people moved to these locations on the basis of authentic trust – through the exercise of personal choice and self-interest – validated by the commodity trust given them by the post-code. Once there they enjoyed strong network trust arising from the shared values of like-minded neighbours. They also became part of the nuanced and recondite authority trust that the English middle classes are so good at attaching to the ownership of property and assets. They could justifiably feel they had arrived.

Like the biblical Assyrians coming down like a wolf on the fold, incoming bank employees suddenly burst into this settled and predictable social orthodoxy, disrupting it forever in an instant. Long-established neighbourhoods changed almost overnight. Young IT professionals, incredibly highly paid in terms of the regional economy, their buying power boosted by relocation allowances and the bank's low-mortgage golden handcuffs, bought property twenty or thirty years in advance of when the market would have hitherto predicted. The cats were well and truly among the pigeons. And, like the sociologists, estate agents too had a field day thanks to this ghettoization in reverse.

Following the bank's move, the collaborative gentility that had neatly balanced public and private trust locally became replaced by an altogether more pragmatic and cynical world-view. As a result of this microcosmic shift, prevailing trust dynamics were never to be the same again.

The Good and the Bad

It can be argued (and probably will be argued by the sentimental visionaries of a misty England of long shadows at summer cricket grounds, anvils, red telephone boxes, yeoman farmers and Sunday morning maiden aunts cycling across the common from thatched cottage to church door) that the outcome reflects an absolute and general diminution of public trust, even, to some extent, raising questions about authentic trust itself.

But despite a host of so-called natural laws describing ways in which the bad always inevitably drives out the good, the notion that there can be good trust and bad trust is a non-starter. Trust exists or else it is absent – that's all. When trust exists it follows the patterns set out in our model. Once it exists it brings power and leverage along with it and makes the little known facts of business life a little better known.

Challenging Orthodoxies

Crucially, the message is that the more systems tend towards orthodoxy, the less they become able to tolerate the possibility of change,
the less flexible they get and the more they become exposed to a
single point of failure. Orthodoxies can choose to ignore little known
facts. As a result, orthodoxy, in whatever context it is found, gives
rise to defensive strategies. The implications of this for trust, collaboration and radical risk strategies are significant.

Think of the trust implications, for example, of a wagon train
drawn into a defensive circle in the old days of the Wild West. The
social dynamics of the bank's new home town meant that people
were probably a little less belligerent towards the circling intruders
than the Native Americans were to the settlers. The same forces
nevertheless were at play. And, if the good burghers had had their
way, there can be little doubt that the upshot would have been the
equivalent of the Apaches breaking into the circle of pioneer wagons.

Not all invasions are successful of course, and not all successful
invasions enjoy immediate success. Sometimes the circle of wagons
holds out for a long time – Ladysmith was eventually relieved, for
example, and Leningrad at length survived – both with their orthodoxies intact. But determined invaders invariably succeed one way
or another – both these relieved cities ultimately succumbed – and
the orthodoxy is shattered.

Change is always inevitable. The ramifications of hijacked Boeings
flying into the walls of the World Trade Center on 11 September
2001 are without question infinitely more far reaching than those
caused by a 24-year-old programmer buying an expensive house next
door to a retired solicitor. The trust dynamics though are much the
same.

From Byzantium to the High Street

From its beginnings in the fourth century of the Common Era, determined invaders took until 1453 – more than eleven centuries – to
finally crush the Byzantine empire. Despite the time it took, the fall
proved not to be the end of history that legend had predicted. The
cycle of rise, decline and fall is still very much with us.

For example, in the days when supermarket tins of beans carried a price sticker and not a barcode, Kwik Save became and remained one of the UK's most successful food retailers. It was a somewhat down-market, cheap-end discounter that lived cheek by jowl with the supermarket giants of the day. Its business model reflected the Pareto dynamics of the giants' operations – eighty per cent of Sainsbury's sales being accounted for by twenty per cent of its product lines. Kwik Save made this twenty per cent its full offering, resulting in maybe an absolute maximum of 1500 products in all, with most of its stores running with 800–1000.

Kwik Save's trust proposition was to offer shoppers these 800 or so products – called KVIs (known value items) – at the lowest possible prices. Discount shoppers are pretty canny customers. Quite literally, they shop around. And they know their KVIs as intimately as any of the retailers. When it comes to radical collaboration strategies with knowledgeable customers, KVIs are up there with the very best.

For a time Kwik Save's operations were wonderfully successful. Its returns per square foot of floor space were the highest in the industry. And while the giants competed head-on in a high-cost, high-risk attempt at gaining market share and going further and further up-market, Kwik Save concentrated on keeping its cost of sales as the very lowest. For example, far from encouraging – and consequently having to appropriately pay – top quality management talent, Kwik Save used its managers as little more than key holders and floor-sweepers. Store merchandising planning was done centrally. And crucially, Kwik Save also removed the huge cost of price marking (sticking price labels on tins and jars) by developing a radical system of price bands that checkout staff were then taught to memorize.

Their wagons in a circle, the orthodoxy of English retailing (notoriously inefficient in world terms and discreetly colluding to maintain absurdly high margins) held that when it came to discount operations, Kwik Save was the very best. Then EEC (the European Economic Community, forerunner of today's EU) regulations shifted and the continental discounters, highly efficient at a fraction of orthodox UK margins, hit town. Practically overnight the high street began to change. When the dust settled Kwik Save had all but disappeared and the game suddenly had new rules.

The shakeout of UK retailing has been radical and shows little sign of slowing down. The survivors and thrivers have been forced to work more closely with their business partners – to replace their exploitive supply-chain mentality with a culture of value chains and to further extend value chains into trust chains that include the customer. A radical departure indeed.

A Byzantine Coda

'Worldly wisdom,' J. M. Keynes, the trust guru, wrote in 1936, 'teaches us that it is better for reputation to fail conventionally than to succeed unconventionally'. From the viewpoint of both success and failure, there is an aspect of the late Kwik Save trust proposition that should be noted, if for no other reason than it widened the circle of wagons of worldly wisdom for all of us. And in a most unconsidered way.

By the same token that cities have leafy and salubrious locations that incoming bankers might choose to ghettoize, they also have some pretty unsalubrious inner-city neighbourhoods that are effectively no-go areas, devoid of any sort of trust for outsiders and where, in the parlance of the golf club, local rules apply.

It was Kwik Save's view that people living in these areas needed their KVIs as much as everyone else – probably more so when the spending patterns of households with small disposable incomes are analysed. They also, of course, represented a lucrative long-term market opportunity. But building and operating stores in areas where respect for life was low and respect for property lower, where even the police thought twice about going in, in less than threes, was a huge challenge.

Finding a solution led Kwik Save to an understanding of the little known facts of business life. Even in the very worst of locations, in places where the half-life of an enterprise could be measured in hours, Kwik Save let it be known that it was prepared to open up shop provided the locals allowed it to and provided suitable, mutually acceptable arrangements could be agreed upon. The point has been made earlier that in order to best manage risk by means of collaborative strategies it is important to discard as much orthodoxy as possible. By doing so, Kwik Save, and its shoppers, together managed the ghetto-risk.

Principled Talk and Engagement in Action

Once the trust choice was made then straightway the talk between the parties became based on a shared understanding of what had to be done *together*. By its openness and willingness to negotiate with some of the toughest characters in some of the toughest corners of the country and by its ability to make, stick to and deliver the unlikeliest mutually beneficial collaborative deals, Kwik Save, for a time, traded in places where no other stores could have survived. Over time, its pioneering work set standards that other retailers could build on. In doing so, it was able to embed and extend network trust in places where trust had hitherto been as foreign as Zanzibar. And the little-known facts of business life became slightly less little known.

5

Radical Strategies for Networks of Values

Communicating Across Values

When people operate in a network cemented by network trust we see an identification of the individual with the group. To be part of a group is to share values with the others to some extent. This sharing of values allows certain things to be said which otherwise cannot be said. To the extent that you find what I am saying here strange, part of the effect is down to the groups and their values that I identify with and that you do not.

As soon as we have groups we have insiders and outsiders. There appears to be a basic human instinct to form groups on the flimsiest of pretexts and to exclude outsiders from the group. Network trust is then built up to allow the group to operate as a group – deliver economies of scale, open up access to commons etc. Many management games explore these effects. Very often when an insider tries to address an outsider, the content of the message is completely lost because all the outsider can hear is the strangeness of the insider's values and the reinforcement of the exclusion. This effect is common when Americans address Europeans.

When we see this operate at a business level, the network concerned is often the organization. The organization can be tightly knit with a strong sense of what it stands for, and although this can be a fine thing, it can also be a severe problem. If customers or suppliers, for instance, regard the organization as a closed group, then communication will become difficult. Often service-level agreements and terms and conditions are a legalistic way of trying to communicate something in these relationships where the basic communication has failed because of these effects. Notice that these mechanisms belong to the world of commodity trust since very often the external manifestation of network trust is commodity trust.

The other typical business scenario is where a professional feels more akin to his professional body than to the organization he works within. Here values are shared and trust is built primarily with the professional body, leading to communication difficulties with the rest of the business organization. Consider, for instance, a negotiation between an accountant and a senior manager about the nature of the accounts and what they are intended to communicate. There is every chance of the conversation degenerating into what seems to be a meaningless set of platitudes and conventionalities.

So certain things rely on network trust in order to be said at all, but at the same time the network trust contributes to the difficulty of communicating these things to anyone else. Despite all our addiction to trying to be objective in what we say, everything is underpinned by our values, and when our values differ from those of others the messages can sound very strange. Attempts to get over this effect lead at best to the formation of new in-groups of people who share new values and who can understand, and out-groups of people to whom this is another puzzling and bizarre twist. Very often improving trust and communication locally can make problems elsewhere.

Network Risk

As often as not the values that underpin a network are implicit and not explicit. To make them explicit requires authentic trust, which is not usually available. The buried values and hidden assumptions that result are the root of the communication difficulties above. It is not immediately apparent why the same utterance is understood by one person and not by another. In popular culture this is represented by the riposte 'Who's asking?'

What is at risk when network trust is challenged is the network itself. To explore the buried values and the hidden assumptions is to challenge the group that holds them, no matter how carefully we try to explain that that is not the intention. When authentic trust is challenged, the person who extended that trust can deal with the challenge as they see fit. But network trust cannot be owned and is defensive in its nature.

One thing that can happen when a group is challenged is that a leader emerges or is thrown up to carry the fight. This can lead to a transmutation from network trust to authority trust, in which case to question or challenge the leader is to challenge the group, and the group lets go of the simple identification with the group to pick up a more antagonistic and purposive identity around the leader.

Always in understanding risk we need to identify the vision or mission that is at risk. Networks, even when they acquire leaders, have no vision or mission. The risk acts on the network and cannot be managed because it has not actively been taken.

> If you don't know where you are trying to go then there is not much risk that you will fail to make your destination.

Despite this, it is possible to have a business vision and to build a team around it. If this is handled well, then the trust basis will be authentic and people will be able to make their own distinctive contribution to the team. If the process is more seductive and less explicit than that, then some combination of authority trust in the leader and network trust in the team will establish itself, with consequences for how the team relates to the outside world. Most military teams, for example, have a very limited range of modes of engagement with the outside world and are very quick to defend themselves against any sort of criticism.

Commodity Risk to Network Trust

We have said that the external face of a network is often a commodity. If an organization produces some commodity products or services and the customers choose to find fault with them, then this is often perceived as an attack on the network (until it becomes routine, when it is seen as a manifestation of the strange values outsiders have). This is the worst face of business, when, for all the 'customer is always right' mantras, actually the customer is always wrong. To complain about the product is to attack the group and that is automatically wrong. The nature of the complaint is not relevant. We see this rather often where an inauthentic bleating about service and brand struggles to hide a deeply rooted belief in the unworthiness of customers to use the product. These are two sides of a coin and reinforce each other strongly.

The Case of the Engineering Process Run Amok

Several colleagues of mine joined a start-up company which made network planning systems for mobile telephone networks. In a rising market this company could do no wrong financially speaking and soon my colleagues were paper millionaires from the share scheme they were part of. As with many such companies, there was a strong core of product ideas from the initial entrepreneurial phase, but when it came to maintaining systems for a wide customer base the management structure of the company needed to change. They were regularly getting beaten up by their powerful customers and yet they knew if they became simply reactive to these pressures they would lose any ability to develop the planning tool.

Being engineers, they believed that the solution lay in the software development process, and being cash-rich they believed that any solution could be bought. So they bought people and consultancy and tools and training and processes. Their belief appeared to be that if they had the best possible development process, then by definition they were doing the best that could be done for their customers. The result was chaotic. If they didn't know how to do something they would make a plan for how they would become able to do it. And if they didn't know how to do that they would make a pre-plan for how to make a plan. Pre-pre-pre-plans had been spotted.

The engineering process was, of course, covering for customer relationships. Nobody would make decisions about how to deal with the pressure from customers and nobody would rock the boat internally because all the paper millionaires wanted to get to a stage where they could sell their shares. We might ask ourselves what we would have done as a customer of such a business!

Devices, Commodities and Networks

We have developed the concept that network trust divides different groups as well as unifying the groups themselves. And we have already explored the notion that network trust can divide the understandings of producers and consumers, suppliers and customers. To round out this analysis, we want to join it with Borgmann's concept of devices.

When we consume something without having any knowledge of or concern for its production, we are in the device paradigm. I neither know nor care how the electricity I am consuming as I sit here at my screen got here. I have no reason not to choose the minimum price supplier and I expect them to maintain 100% reliability. The retailing of commodities of all sorts tends to this model, although other models are available. There are restaurants where customers are educated in the exact provenance of their food and the intricacies and constraints on its production as part of the experience of eating good food. (Some schoolchildren study the delivery chain of the food on offer in their own canteens as part of an enlightened education process.) From our perspective of network trust, we can see the device paradigm and commoditization acting to break the connections between the groups of people on either side of the divide.

The device paradigm says precisely that it is no concern of customers of a sports shop if the footballs they buy are made using child labour. And if the customers want to get into a conversation about such issues that cross the divide, it is likely to be confrontational and not collaborative. This model from a supplier's perspective says that we want customers and we want to please our customers but we will never speak to them about our concerns and they must not take an interest in our internal processes. In other words, they can buy our commodity but they cannot become part of our network.

It wasn't always so. The first home my wife and I had after we were married was in a picturesque village, complete with medieval Buttercross, in the countryside to the south of the town we worked in. Every week, the village butcher's shop would put up a chart covering

> half the wall detailing the life stories of the animals the meat from which was on sale within. They'd line their shop windows with photographs of the beasts and rosettes they'd won at shows. The butcher would proudly tell you the exact and entire provenance of any cut you wanted. You couldn't buy a pie or a sausage in the shop without getting chapter and verse of what was in it, where it was raised, what it had for breakfast even. Very often the unchanged fields in which the animals had spent their entire lives were within a stone's throw of the shop. You could even go and talk to the farmer and see the present generation animals strolling in the same fields. That was long ago. We sometimes go back to visit the old place. The ancient Buttercross still stands proudly at the village's main junction. It's quainter than ever now – full of exclusive, up-market executive homes built on the very ground that used to feed their food, and priced to keep out underachievers. Nowadays the village is a device for living and its people buy their meat at Tesco.

By deliberately fostering the separation of these two groups, we ensure that their values diverge and that they cannot be heard by each other. Consider the car salesman whose every utterance is discounted by every customer, or the ubiquitous replacement window salesperson on the telephone. In the end, the extreme inauthenticity of these communications can only lead to disaster. When people try to recover some authenticity from these situations we get other strange anomalies.

So without stereotyping people or having prejudices about them, I can have a conception of them that is clearly a shell or an abstraction of who they are. It will be dominated by some context or other – they are a fellow parent from school or a work colleague or a shop assistant or a cold-calling telephone canvasser. If we are suddenly thrown into another context – perhaps someone is mugged in the street – then my sense of who the other person is and how they may behave is most likely of very little use. We may even not recognize people whom we see very often in one context when we see them in another.

In business terms this becomes an issue for branding, because the boundaries between brands must to some extent reflect the expected and contextual boundaries. As a business I do not expect to get stationery and accountancy from the same supplier. The services I offer must fit some initial preconception of things that other businesses might buy and might see as a rounded offering. But in the business context too, things may change, do change as part of the logic of doing business. Today's collaborator is tomorrow's competitor and vice versa. Yesterday's bookseller is today's source of discounted business software.

I was involved in the mid-1990s in a project looking into the feasibility of privatizing government-run factories in Egypt. I had responsibility for Alexandria. Among the government's extensive operations in the city were a number of antique factories – factories that made antiques (technologically they were also antiques themselves, of course). Any irony associated with the notion of factory-made antiques was totally lost so my report took a different tack. Individually and collectively, the factories were perfect candidates for management buy-outs. They had extensive marketing operations based on family connections throughout Europe and North America, generating lots of profitable business. As so often in Egypt, it was politics that decided things in the end, and as far as I know the factories are still run by civil servants. That aside, the opportunity to be part of the process by which reified devices – antiques – were delivered to unencumbered consumers was a real privilege. For order tracking we implemented a version of the traceability that in those days formed part of ISO 9000. We used the output, suitably printed up on papyrus complete with hieroglyphics, as a charter of authenticity and provenance. And so the ancient traditions of an English Buttercross village were transplanted to Alexandria and history itself became a device.

So basing a business relationship on the content of what it delivers, services, supplies, sales – whatever – is to base it on something provisional, secondary. If we set ourselves up to manage the purchase of stationery we may get good at doing so but completely fail to recognize when that is not what we need to do in this particular relationship. By putting a particular frame on the purpose of the relationship, we will be systematically blind to other possibilities. This will be unimportant until the day when it is crucial.

We recognize that brands represent a major asset for their owners (they can, after all be bought and sold for large sums). We also recognize that risk to brands is now a major concern. Something worth billions one day can be trashed by some unfortunate associations and poor handling of the press the next. This is only a special case of the general rule that to abstract the company image and function into a shell or a reputation that stands in for the company in its transactions puts the real thing, the company, at risk from damage to the abstraction. In today's world people increasingly know how to attack those abstractions and how to subvert their meanings.

The alternative is to base company relationships explicitly in the relationship itself, which can then be reviewed for its contribution to the well-being of both parties, for joint opportunities and risks. In this situation there cannot be damage propagated through from abstractions and projections because these are understood to be the tools of the relationship. When something changes dramatically it is immediately the subject of attention and there is nothing that cannot in principle be turned to advantage. Logically relationships handled this way are 'strategic relationships', but the literature on these fails to understand the dynamics implicit in different styles of relating.

Commodity Trust, Hierarchies, Pyramids and Sharp Operators

It seems simple. I want to supply you with some goods. (So from the outset we have the kind of coincidence of wants that is at the heart of the barter arrangements that preceded money. We have argued elsewhere that this arrangement actually still exists, i.e. that money is the commodity of barter.) If these goods are basically a commodity – that is, they are items of a known value – to you then I need to get the price of the goods down in order to generate value for you. So since you don't really care where the goods come from, I do what I need to do to get them to you at a price that is competitive. The deal I have with you is that you don't ask too many questions and I look after your (price) interests. I don't question whether you really need the commodity I supply and you don't question the practices I use in order to get you a good price. This is commodity trust.

This deal does not take place in isolation. It is surrounded by a context in which I have to sell lots and lots of the commodity in order to generate the buying muscle needed to get the price down with my suppliers. I have to take commercial risks in the expansion and the marketing that this deal implies. If we are talking about potatoes as a commodity then at least I can see them, and the demand for them is based on hunger for chips – a reasonably stable phenomenon. If we are talking about shares as a commodity then this is no longer grounded in the same way. A share is largely a social creation that has few intrinsic properties. (Markets would disagree, of course, and claim that the intrinsic value of a share had two dimensions: one, it represented some fraction of the firm's overall assets, and two, it represented indefinite future cash flow from dividends. Arguably it isn't the share itself here that's the underpinning commodity in pyramids so much as share ownership, which is the true virtual construct.)

So we start with commodity trust around the sale of some commodities that are well grounded (the shares themselves?) and quickly move to sets of commercial deals and financial arrangements that appear to have similar properties but are actually only analogous to the trading of agricultural produce (the share ownership derivative?). In a pyramid selling scheme, we dispense altogether with the commodity and sell the right to sell to others in the scheme, take the pickings and escape. Of course, pyramid selling schemes are illegal and grossly exploitative of people at the base of the pyramid, but that does not seem to prevent them from working. Pyramid selling is the ultimate commodity trust application, where the promise of riches from the scheme is the sole product in the scheme. In the normal commercial case there is a mixture of grounded trading and what we could call derivative trading that sits on top of it in pyramid fashion. From inside these complex trading systems it is very difficult to distinguish grounded from free-floating trading: ultimately there may be no meaningful operational distinction.

If a company such as a supermarket operator manages to build a successful business and generate commodity trust with its customers, then it will also generate good prices for shares in the company.

Classic Example

Kwik Save took the 20% of products that accounted for 80% of the business of Tesco and Sainsbury and made it the entire product range, labelling each product a KVI – a known value item.

This is a bit like pyramid selling – the KVI commodity overlaying the Kwik Save commodity. It was totally successful before there was competition, as we have written elsewhere.

It appears that a high share price is only what is deserved given the commercial performance of the company. The shares are the basis of a commodity trust deal with shareholders (which is compromised when fancy share deals, rights and scrip issues, used for short-term financing, dilute share values as described above). The shareholders are interested not in absolute value but in growth, so the money available via the share price must be invested in the company to improve its performance still further. (The commodity though, as traded, is second hand and as such not directly grounded in raising capital for the firm.) When sentiment in the stock market changes and the share price falls, the shareholders look to the company management to reverse their fortunes, but of course the share price is outside the control of the management in this situation. The commodity trust deal was not grounded in a way that allows trust to be rebuilt easily. The phenomenon of appetite for shares is different from the phenomenon of appetite for chips.

The packaging of tradable goods into commodity status is founded on an economic model of trading where knowledge of the specifics of the exchange and the goods concerned are discounted. The fact that this potato is different in many ways from that potato is not germane to the price or the physical movement of potatoes if we are talking generic potatoes. Commodity trust says I don't care which potato and you can use my lack of interest to generate a price-efficient deal. There is a hierarchy buried in this scheme because neither the supply nor the consumer purchase of potatoes is decoupled from the market for carrots or, for that matter, joints of beef. The supermarket operators are precisely the management hierarchies that coordinate the economies of scale and the purchasing power across ranges of commodities.

The world trades on the basis of commodity trust. Commodity trust explicitly contains the seeds of its own destruction because it works on the basis of the fewer questions the better and the less content and continuity in the business relationships the better. Like barter, it works when it works and it collapses when it doesn't. End of story.

In a parallel way, the authority trust in the major organizations that service these trading systems is not capable of handling questions about the purpose or procedures of the system – the system works, and POSIWID. So don't rock the boat. This authority is the repository of the commodity trust and is actually hamstrung by that trust. We can hear this whenever the hoary old question is raised about why supermarkets sell poor food that people don't want. And that the argument of the USA is not with the *people* of Iraq . . .

6

A World Running on Network Trust

Social Systems Run on Trust

There is a great unawareness of the level of trust needed to get even the most basic social systems – families, firms, institutions and so on – to run. Even less about keeping them running successfully. In many ways we are inside such social structures and take for granted many of their features. When we come across social systems in other cultures they can appear completely baffling and we perceive them to be weird.

As we have had occasion to say rather often, we see the trust that did exist only after it has been destroyed in some way. The sickening downward spiral in the Balkan wars stands as a paradigm for how much there is to lose. There are areas of business life where people are more focused on making sure others do not succeed than they are on making sure the fundamentals of value creation and sustainability are in place.

The trust equation from this perspective is:

Do I choose to work with those around me to develop a good situation for the group or do I make sure my own position is secure as a primary goal?

Here is a view:

'. . . it's like when the cops get a pay rise.'

'Uh?'

'When the cops get a pay rise they all get it don't they? Whether they deserve it or not – the good cop, the bad cop. You see, people always get it wrong when they think that people in the same line will get together to sort things out for themselves – whether we're talking about cops, melon sellers or anybody. The big problem is the guys who work hard to get things for the group only get the same as they get for everybody else. In the end it ain't worth it. That's why we have Wall Street rip-offs. That's why we have Wall Street period. That's why Union bosses get so rich. That's why folks don't like paying taxes. That's why there soon ain't goin' to be any cops. That's why satisfaction's the only thing worth having . . .' the melon man spoke rapidly, as if he'd like nothing better than talking forever. He paused, 'see what I'm saying?' he said.

'I understand about the cops' pay rise,' Felix admitted, 'as for the rest . . . why's there going to be no more cops soon?'

'Hey don't worry, it won't happen this evening.'

'I'm not worrying . . . I just like understanding that's all.'

The melon man wondered for a second how they'd got to where they were. He was only used to talking to melons. Now he had one answering back, one he had to explain to.

'Look,' he said, 'it's nothing personal . . .'

'. . . I'm not taking it personally,' Felix said, his voice in neutral, 'I told you it doesn't worry me.'

'It's the price of cops see. Folks pay their taxes and they get cops. Cops spread themselves over everybody. Folks begin to think maybe they're not getting what they need from cops – all cops do is squeeze confessions, wait for their pensions and take backhanders – I told you this is nothing personal, there's folks think all dogs do is just shit all over, me – I like dogs. Same thing with cops if you follow my meaning . . .'

'. . . get on with the story why don't you?' Felix said.

'. . . so these folks – the ones thinking they're being ripped off by the price of cops – they get together and buy a security man to guard their own little patch. Before you know it every neighborhood has its own private police force – better value for money see – no sharing. Folks stop paying for the regular cops because they have to share them with everybody. Pretty soon there's no cops. Same with public medicine, public schools, anything folks have to share – you name it. It's Wall Street all over.'

'So I'm a victim of insider dealing am I? A Wall Street casualty?'

'. . . best just forget it.'

Source: *Dead on Time*, John Smith, 1999,
Cliché fiction (Opus 18 No. 2)

When studying these choices and these social system questions, a key observation is the degree to which the factors in this choice are externalized. People often report that they have tried cooperation but that this person, that group or the other external factor – the economy, foreign competition, regulations, the economic climate or whatever – made it impossible. Equally, but typically in more abject circumstances, people may report that everything is against them but that they are a group of people working together to overcome the impossible odds.

It feels to us as though these are the hardest issues we face as social beings. Much of the effort in organizational life goes into fudging these questions by erecting business processes, notions of best practice, standards, principles and so forth, which provide mechanisms for cooperation without addressing the fundamentals. These things work because of our natural socializing and cooperative tendencies. But these things can also be instruments of social betrayal and repression, just as nationalism was in the Balkans. The social motivation will out and people will decide that the purpose of the system is what it does (POSIWID).

If we look at the negative frame of this trust equation it is this:

Is the risk of relying on this group of people supportable and how does it compare with the risk of going it alone and being an outsider?

The more complex a social setting, the more intractable this question is. Not only do we need to decide whether we can trust some group of people but we also need to assess whether they are in a position to hold our trust. They may in turn have their ability to act socially damaged by some other group. It is the web of trust that supports us and there is continuous work to be done to maintain the strength of the web. Individuals and groups try to seize power to isolate themselves from this uncomfortable interdependence and in doing so set up the chains of damage that others need to repair. We have a strong social illusion that there is an overarching vision, or – in business language – a helicopter view, that can allow us to organize the web, but there is no evidence to support these claims. It is the hardest lesson in the world to learn to leave well alone.

One particular way of claiming power is to systematically abuse the existing trust for individual advantage. Experience shows that there will always be people who take this antisocial route to temporary safety.

An Example

Consider a group of women bringing a legal action against a drug company for the effects of the so-called third-generation pill, which they allege gives rise to a propensity to develop blood clots. The women have extensive first- and second-hand experience of what they consider the symptoms to be and of the causal relationship. The drug company concerned has large amounts of money at stake and commands the research agenda (we no longer have even quasi-independent research into such questions). The women rely on the law for redress but the questions of legitimate evidence play into the hands of the drug company. In the end the women denounce very publicly the legal system for its inability to deliver justice. Trust in the legal system, in business ethics, in medical drugs all goes down a notch or two. Irrespective of the substance of the case, this is not the way to build a cooperative society. Everyone is forced (by their own reckoning) to take a defensive position and fight their corner. The leadership to know that this can easily spiral downwards feels rarer as our society gets more complex and more interdependent.

We can frame the basic question again as a dialectic:

> The ability to extend trust from our own resources and for our own reasons contradicts the development of trustworthy social structures.

We need to understand that the business mechanisms that attempt to demonstrate trustworthiness – audits, corporate governance, quality processes, charter marks and so forth – are moves in the social game. Like all 'trust me' moves they are equally capable of confirming distrust as they are of building confidence. The idea that I as a consumer would trust a company because of its structures is laughable, though there are people who go down this route. But a company that can demonstrate that it knows how to use such structures to protect my interest certainly has my trust. The law does not define social justice, but everyone gains strength when it is demonstrated that the law can be used to uphold social justice.

The dialectic lets us feel how radical the risk of trust is. By attacking social structures we risk their destruction. Without attacking social structures they come to betray and repress us. We must learn how to attack in a reforming, socially oriented way, in the name of values that people can identify with. We need to trust the people around us to be bigger than the social structures around us that make life possible. What we mean by 'bureaucratic' as a term of abuse is the structures becoming bigger than the people in them. Management interventions almost never increase the stature of the people in the system.

The social structures we build, including all our business organizations, are ways of promoting trust to allow business to take place. They form an offer of a social and psychological contract. They can go out of their way to respect that contract and to make sure it is suitable or they can exploit it for what it is worth. As organizations grow and age, it can be very difficult to stay in contact with that contract and how it changes over time. What was responsible action can become irresponsible without the nature of the action having changed.

Dynamic Relating

Many of our cultural institutions push us towards static conceptions of people. If I enter into a contract with you, it doesn't matter whether I, you or our circumstances change, the contract still stands, unless it can be shown that the contract was unreasonable given foreknowledge of those changes. The exceptions are *force majeur* situations such as the death or bankruptcy of either party. Similarly, if I am a mail order customer of yours there are some static expectations on both sides – you will keep sending me catalogues and special offers and I will buy something occasionally. This latter relationship can easily become ludicrous: how long does a mail order company think I am likely to have toddler age children?

Big Structures, Little People

Bureaucracy often throws up some strange patterns as people struggle to say one thing while doing another:

One of my daughters brought home from school a letter about the school discipline policy. The letter contained three policy documents that I could not immediately relate to each other. The request was to reply to the governors if there were any problems with the policy. I wrote to the Chair of the governors saying that I didn't have a problem with the policy as far as I could tell but that the documents were not fit for the purpose. I then received a telephone call from the deputy headteacher asking me to withdraw my letter otherwise they would have to call a special meeting of the governors to discuss it.

I guess there was a formal requirement to consult on the discipline policy but that no one was actually supposed to comment. It was probably also true that the practical discipline used had no relation to the formal policy, which was there to meet another requirement. We could also comment that the relationship between the governors and staff was clearly not one of governing except in a formal sense.

> The trust relationships revealed in this scenario are fascinating –
> parents, pupils, staff and governors each trusting each other to deal
> with immediate issues without reference to the set of rules and the
> governance laid down.

We could look at the other side of the coin:

> If I had had a serious problem with the discipline policy that it did
> not suit the staff to address, the formal policy would have been used
> to sideline the issues in a way that left me with no redress. So a
> consultation mechanism involving a large amount of formal communi-
> cation can be used to make sure no actual communication happens
> at all. This is the modern meaning of due diligence.

As we have tried to show throughout, to get real communication to
work there has to be pre-existing trust at the level of the issues to
be communicated.

The Case of the Public 'Joint' Venture

There was (once) a transportation project called CrossRail designed
to establish a new east–west rail link across London. It was jointly
run and staffed by Railtrack (which then ran the rail infrastructure)
and London Underground.

The project was stuck and one of the symptoms was that the IT
provision was perceived to generate no value. In a workshop with the
directors we determined to find out what was wrong by attempting
an important internal project, IT related, and observing the problems.
The issue we chose to work on was cost–time integration of the
programme plan for building the new link. There was a detailed cost
plan and detailed task plan and no way of relating them.

Two events located the problem, without, unfortunately, resolving
it. In a key planning workshop the facilitator was crucified and it became
obvious that Railtrack did task planning and London Underground did

cost planning and coordination was not on the agenda no matter what the directors had in mind.

It was my turn to be crucified next, when over the course of a long train journey I tried to get the Engineering Director to understand that there were two plans – one to build the railway when it got government approval and one to work towards that approval on an annual basis. I was recommending that practical time–cost integration should start now, not at some arbitrary future date. My complete and dismal failure to communicate even some inkling of this issue was an early lesson in the crucial significance of trust.

Let us not be mistaken about this. Many millions of pounds of public funds, the future of a vital piece of infrastructure, hundreds of highly skilled professionals, oversight by Parliament and the Treasury, all beached on the simplest and most obvious thing: the mistrust between two organizations. It wasn't tackled then and remains today in the legacy of Railtrack's failure and the painful privatization of London Underground.

The Paradox

Network trust is a very important and deep paradox. The paradox is this. We know, can prove, that there are much better outcomes available if we can trust each other to keep our commitments. These outcomes can be better for everyone without exception, and we cannot access them. There are just too many opportunities for people to take partisan advantage on the way. People in general want to gain power over others by gaining relatively better outcomes rather than get an absolutely better outcome for themselves that also allows others to win. This is western business culture and it is so dominant that we think it is almost human nature.

In the financial world:

A major bank in a conversation with a colleague said categorically that they would rather lose a million pounds and know where they lost it than have a CEO who led them to fortune without them understanding where it came from.

In the technology world:

> Modern encryption techniques are used to code phone batteries so
> that any batteries other than the manufacturer's own brand discharge
> more rapidly. They are used to quietly downgrade printer resolution
> when someone else's printer cartridges are used. They are going to
> be used to squeeze out the market for free, open source, software.
> Free trade has never meant trade designed to enhance the wealth of
> all the trading partners. Powerful players are able to tilt the terms of
> trade in their own favour.

And in the real world:

> When a distressed 26-year-old Japanese-built, Greek-owned, single-
> hulled tanker, flying a flag of convenience, crewed by Asian seamen,
> chartered by a Singapore firm and carrying 70 000 tonnes of heavy
> crude oil reportedly owned by a Latvian firm, having been refused
> haven to get it under repair, began leaking its cargo off the coast of
> north-west Spain, the response of the authorities was to have it towed
> into international waters. Failing that, into some other country's terri-
> torial waters. West Africa was identified as the ideal location. The
> *Prestige* went down in 3000 metres of water, 170 miles west of Spain's
> Cies Islands, on 19 November 2002, turning her remaining cargo into
> a seabed time-bomb. She left a 70 mile long oil slick and a devastated
> coast line behind her. The tragedy of the commons is played out over
> and over again. A mixture of nationalism, bad science, poor leader-
> ship, lack of trust, poor management and plain greed quickly destroys
> a global resource.

Next time you build a business case, ponder this. There is a much
more powerful, more beneficial business case available if you can get
stable cooperation across a wide enough range of stakeholders. This
business case puts the one you are writing in the shade. You cannot
access that business case however, because you cannot get a set of
trusting relationships together. Someone will betray the rest and take

narrow advantage, leaving you looking silly. Those figures in the case are an admission of failure, of being unable to get the programme established as what people want to cooperate to do.

We make a virtue of talking about the competitive advantage we will gain and the value we will generate that the competition will not. We indulge in macho talk about making things happen, but really we are just strutting. Our opposition in getting things to happen is a bunch of others trying to get their programmes to happen, instead or as well.

In the wake of the major health scares and food scandals in the UK, I attended a meeting of industry experts and representatives of the major companies involved in the supply chain in the UK. The meeting was about traceability and other approaches to improving food safety. The meeting was called by the relevant government department, the Food Standards Agency. In the whole meeting no one put the consumer viewpoint. No one said 'well we owe people at least this level of information and responsiveness in the event of a problem'. It was all a piece of positioning to do the minimum without being outflanked by anyone else.

7

Building Network Trust in an Adversarial World

Whatever the context, I have to be concerned at a chapter entitled 'building' any sort of trust. Everyone does. I have to be concerned because it is an invitation to misread, to take a utilitarian view that here is an expert's recipe for trust and, once built, trust is there for the using. All our experience of business says that this doesn't work. People understand the difference between authentic trust as a gift and inauthentic collusion and seduction prior to exploitation. We have all been through it too many times. When it comes to trust we're all experts.

But building trust is a life's work. Building trust allows the only real security we will ever know. It is the source of creativity and of joy. It is empowering (to try to rescue another long-suffering word). What is it like though, to try to establish trust in the midst of endemic mistrust?

An Adversarial Context

Business is an adversarial thing. The economic model western society has adopted gives at first the appearance of thriving on competition. It rewards and loves winners. It destroys and abuses losers. To a large extent, it's a zero-sum game in which what's won is what's lost. Too often, though, too much is at stake to trust outcomes to competition. This is the fear at the heart of the groups where network trust is found. It's where collusion begins and where its power is derived.

And it's not just business. A pretty compelling case can be made quite readily for adversarialism being the basic building block of society itself. As well as business, parliament, the media and the law all have adversarial hearts. And whatever 'checks and balances' fancy wrappers it comes in, adversarialism is barely one step up from the law of the jungle. It's a harsh and inhospitable place to try to build trust, that's for sure. That, nevertheless, is the challenge – to take trust over the boundaries of adversarialism. Here's a good place to start:

> We know of no occasion on which subterfuge has been successfully used against us.
> > Quotation, purporting to be from an FBI report.
> > A chapter header in Norman R. Augustine's
> > famous book, *Augustine's Law*.

Whether or not it's true, it's easy to laugh at the mentality behind writing such a sentence, or even behind expressing such a sentiment by any means of articulation. The bureaucratic–adversarial mind is a wondrous thing, deserving of much study. Its wonder was magnified many-fold by the Cold War's adversarialism, when the enemy was a bogey-man lurking round every corner and the Bureau was there to protect us. But, hubris and self-satisfaction aside, the quotation reflects pretty accurately the way in which, thanks to adversarialism, we demand that our expectations are met. It is the equivalent of an Andersen-audited revenue stream in Enron's final accounts. Or the project champion's sign-off on a bit of software testing. Or approving boardroom nods for the CFO's projections. It is the public face of the trusted institution. It's what we want to hear.

So there are lots of trust implications behind the quotation. Its mere existence is a clear enough indication that what passes for trust between the institution and the people it is intended to serve has been compromised and is in all probability fatally flawed. For example, if the writers truly believe it, then they've got to be really dumb to write it down. Either that or there's some other agenda in play.

Augustine doesn't tell us, but maybe the quotation goes on to say something like:

. . . yet we have five fully documented instances in which we have successfully used subterfuge against the CIA or NSA . . .

. . . or some other adversarial agency with which the FBI are in competition for headlines and resources.

That said, it is clear that the aims of the quotation's author include fostering trust and proving to those payrolling the operation that they are getting value for money. Trust for bucks so to speak, as though it were a buyable and sellable commodity. Those issues aside, probably the most important role the quotation has is that of being a 'trust marker' in an adversarial world.

Trust Markers: Milestones on the Road to Abuse

Trust markers are things – quotations, bits of knowledge, stories, soundbites – that are in the public domain and that are generally held to be not (yet) proven to be untrue (it's an adversarial world, remember). An adversary reinforces a current trust stance by pointing to a trust marker that has previously been laid down. In doing so, the cause of trust is further fostered. That is the intention, at any rate. Political manifestos are classic trust markers – milestones to nowhere, as often as not.

In Enron's case we're talking about previous years' published accounts, reports of exceptional growth and a record of rising share prices. In Andersen's case there are any number of reliable trust markers stretching from hundreds of other Enron-like blue-chips, and stretching even as far back into the mists of history as the so-called 'conventions' of the accountancy profession – the consistency, caution, conservatism and so forth – on which the whole charade is based.

In the FBI's case, there's still probably Al Capone to count as a success. In other words, in McLuhan's immortal words, the medium is once again the message. Never was this insight better illustrated than with trust markers. Press releases, year-end figures, prospectuses, contracts, business plans – you name it, they all deliver a self-referential basis for lying or supporting lies.

Adversarialism still rules, though, even when it comes to trust markers. The problem is summed up concisely – and authentically – in the following snippet of news:

> ITV Digital has reached its final humiliation, as the punch-line of every joke. Yesterday Lord Williams of Mostyn, the libel QC turned dapper leader of the House of Lords, parried reporters' questions with ease at a press gallery lunch at Westminster. Having talked of the virtues of freedom of expression, he avoided answering any questions on hunting or Lords reform by saying 'If you move to "on the record" discussions, no one can really tell the truth.' Pressed by a journalist from Carlton, Lord Williams illustrated his point by asking the journalist for his own views on the Carlton and Granada liability to the Football League over the ITV Digital fiasco. Silence.
>
> City Diary, *The Guardian*, 11 April 2002

We have long been encouraged to trust the freedom of the press and assured that journalists keep their readers' best interests at heart at all times. They do so by playing their insurmountable trust marker card at every opportunity, with the question:

'Why is this lying bastard lying to me?'

Newspapers maintain the question is the foundation of their relationships with readers. The question's purpose is to establish trust while its very articulation makes trust impossible. This makes Lord Williams's reply into a pretty compelling trust issue.

'Because no one can really tell the truth.'

That this is so even amid the mere trivia of a misguided business venture points up a powerful network trust irony. There's an old business cliché that goes something like 'no one ever got rich by overestimating the public's taste'. The corollary is that the way to get rich is to pitch at the lowest common denominator of taste. Trust the public's lack of discernment. It works, of course, from fast-food franchises, through the tabloid press to soft-porn TV. With ITV

Digital, however, things seem to have changed: the cliché seems to have been stood on its head.

ITV Digital's business model was to buy up second-level football matches, on the premise that couch-potato fans would snap up its digital set-top boxes and pay-to-view contracts. The fans would have their TV football and the Carlton–Granada link-up would have a captive market forever more. And hey presto, it's welcome to the brave new world of digital TV. In the event, ITV Digital had so few viewers that analysis showed it would have been cheaper for it to have taken each one to the game in a chauffeur-driven limo, given them £500 spending money and put them up overnight in a five star hotel before chauffeuring them back home the next day after a slap-up lunch. The major trust marker in all of this was the £380 million deal struck between the TV firm and the football clubs. Financial pressures brought about by the optimistic unreality of the sums – pounds and viewers alike – trashed the deal. Careers and share values crashed, football clubs went into administration and the mighty giants of digital TV were forced into a defensive merger.

The implications of network trust clashing with a commodified football product and a commodified couch-potato market are still being played out. The owners of the Premiership are looking forward with trepidation to renegotiating their deal with the sole remaining digital TV giant. And the FA, feeling the fall-out, is looking for a new CEO following the incumbent's resignation, with equal trepidation.

'No one can really tell the truth' is a salutary lesson when it comes to trust markers wherever they are found. That they still exist and still exert influence over trust issues only illustrates the power of the 'medium' being the 'message'. In essence it exemplifies the 'public-ness' that we instinctively hide behind whenever there is a failure of trust.

In the highly adversarial world of investment banking for example, 'Chinese Walls' is the colourful metaphor for a trust marker. Chinese Walls are intended to separate market analysts and bankers from each other and prevent cross-contamination. The implicit vastness and the stony impenetrability of the Great Wall of China are there to assure the investor of the accuracy, independence and integrity of market information while at the same time providing assurances that the bank itself has no financial axe to grind regarding the analysis.

Or not. On the same day Lord Williams was making his 'no one can really tell the truth' confession, New York state attorney general Eliot Spitzer delivered a report following a ten-month investigation into the *fin de siècle* dotcom bubble and its subsequent collapse.

Focusing on the role played in the fiasco by bankers Merrill Lynch, Spitzer described his findings as "a shocking betrayal of trust by one of Wall Street's most respected names".

Basically what Spitzer revealed was that, Chinese Walls or not, analysts right across Wall Street had 'talked-up' dotcom stocks for which their own banking colleagues were earning huge fees arranging market capitalization and IPOs. No puffs, no fees was the rule.

Knowledge is power and power relationships are easily exploited, the more so in an adversarial context. While these analysts were bombarding the market with buy signals, their internal emails told a different story:

> 'Piece of junk' one 'buy' stock was described as in October 2000.

> 'Nothing interesting about this except banking fees' said another in January 2001.

Throughout its entire life Enron exploited a similar power relationship although in a subtly different way. There was great competition among newspapers for the billions of Enron advertising bucks. The deal was that ads would only be placed in papers whose city pages were totally bullish about the entire Enron project. This meant writing-up not only its growth projections, its diversification plans and its business model, but also its leadership, its global reach, its happy band of stock-owning employees and its increasing political power as a world player. Following the crash, the papers involved are still exploring ways of rebuilding their integrity and regaining their readers' trust. Many Enron stakeholders are exploring ways of rebuilding their lives.

The old business maxim that *what gets rewarded gets done* ensured Enron got its way in return for spending millions of advertising dollars on page after page of glossy pull-outs. In turn, these ads augmented the pile of worthless trust markers on which the Enron empire was built.

In terms of trust, adversarialism can be seen as having certain characteristics. Bear in mind that trust implies motivation to cooperate, ideally, but not necessarily, with someone or some body that has our best interests at heart. So, in the adversarial world these players inhabit, we cooperate with Merrill Lynch and Enron by subscribing to their services – often when they are or were a monopoly supplier, either through exclusive access to a stock in the case of Merrill Lynch or by a regional monopoly in the case of Enron.

> 'What if everyone thought that way?'
> 'Then I'd be stupid to think any different, wouldn't I?'
> Yossarian's world view, from *Catch-22*,
> Joseph Heller

Radical Trust Strategies in an Adversarial World

Trust is more fundamental than power – power, after all, stems from the levers of trust – and many stories tell how power overreaches and subverts itself. We have to deal with power but we may also want to know whether a situation is well-founded in terms of trust as a fundamental. To do so we merely need to make ourselves aware of the local demands of power and understand the degree to which trust is displaced and disabled by those demands.

Try putting a clause to that effect in a contract and taking it to your bank when you're negotiating a loan and see where it gets you. Try negotiating accredited supplier status with Shell or Tesco in those terms and the rules of the power games will rapidly be brought into play.

Despite its Mary Poppins tones, that sentiment is precisely what is at the heart of trust analysis. And even the most purblind trust analysis would have stopped Enron in its tracks, saved Andersen's reputation and maintained Merrill Lynch's integrity.

Simply by answering the question 'how authentic is the public persona I have to adopt to cooperate with these guys?' and the corollary 'how would I expect these guys to operate if that's how I have to be?' it would have been impossible for things to continue as they did.

Trust, as with motivation, requires that you treat me as I am, not as you want me to be. And that's the challenge – there are an awful lot of people around. Treating them all as individuals is impractical for a business operation, and treating them as they are is totally impossible. Despite what this implies about 'the customer is always right', great things are nonetheless achievable.

Cooperation issues come and go all the time. Some last mere seconds; others are the work of a lifetime. Adversarialism – really another word for choice and its presentation – is ever present and comes in many shapes and sizes: are you with the Israelis or the Palestinians? Does your business use Sun or Microsoft? Do you take coffee regular or decaff? Do you trust your customers or not? Which political party do you support? Are you pro-abortion or anti-abortion? Are you with us or against us? The aim of adversarialism, wherever possible, is to reduce everything to a simple, controllable binary choice – yes or no, guilty or not guilty, profit or loss – it leaves no space for trust. Its intensity depends on what's at stake.

Contrast this with what we earlier called engagement in which we look for an understanding of what we need to do *together* to get to where we need to go. Exploring the impact of what's at stake in this – as well as drawing a picture of the scope of what is involved – is where our model comes in. Engagement means always looking at the four dimensions we have set out.

Following a decision or some significant event, we are all used to what is generally called 'coming to terms' with the situation that results. Exploring 'coming to terms' is a good opportunity to revisit the basics of the model.

Say, for example, our firm becomes part of the supply chain of an industry giant, Shell, for instance, or Tesco. What is it we have to come to terms with in terms of cooperative behaviour? Or else a firm gets taken over and has to become part of the culture of its new owners. Or else a firm joins an industry best practice body or seeks certification for some of its processes. Or an individual considers joining a religious sect or embarking on a new relationship. 'Coming to terms' examples are countless.

Whatever is happening, there are four ways in which our motivations to cooperate need to be considered – personal, security, commodity and authority. These are at once similar – they are all faces of the same thing ultimately – and all different in as much as they have the definite, definable drivers we have set out. These four dimensions define the scope available to us in which to build trust.

Personal trust is the cooperative behaviour we bring to a situation through choice and self-interest. Very often the adversarial nature of the situations with which we have to come to terms do not leave too many choices open to us. In the end we settle for an acceptable level of public behaviour and demeanour – the publicness referred to above – which may or may not be entirely in keeping with our preferences but which is satisfactory.

Network or security trust reflects the social and business networks and ties that provide the contexts for our personal and working lives. Very often, the public face we adopt reflects paying the price of membership of the groups we belong to. The implications of this are inescapable. For example, it is virtually impossible to be a fully functioning member of UK society without being a property owner. Property ownership implies a neighbourhood. Neighbourhoods have rules aimed at maintaining property values. Similarly, it is unheard of for a blue-chip listed firm to be audited by anyone outside the 'big four' accountancy firms.

Commodity trust is a measure of what we are prepared to forgo in terms of freedom of choice to satisfy our sense of duty or responsibility. In terms of the religious example cited above, it implies following whatever dietary laws or dress codes the religion sets out for its followers. In terms of the industry giants it implies adherence to and faith in the brand as a means of delivering earnings per share.

Authority trust reflects the willingness with which we submit to the decision making of those who have power over us. It implies some imposition – imposed or constrained choice and a fear of sanction for not conforming. This dimension is at the heart of power relationships – papers submitted to Enron for fear of the sanction of losing advertising dollars; Merrill Lynch analysts complied with Merrill Lynch bankers for fear of the bank next door getting the business. To an extent the first two can be seen as dimensions of behaviour, the second two as dimensions of control. Whatever its context, these are the dimensions within which trust has to develop. They define the scope of the challenge. They show us what 'coming to terms' actually involves.

The question then arises, how exactly is trust built? The answer is that trust to some extent already exists otherwise nothing at all would be happening. So the question more properly becomes, how can trust be improved and built upon? The answer begins with using engagement to challenge the prevailing conventional wisdom. For the aristocrats of Aragon this might entail a rewrite of their pledge to the king:

> We, who are as good as you only having less power, agree to cooperate fully with you, who are no better than us, in exercising power over us, providing you acknowledge and aspire, through engagement, to meet our needs in respect of personal, security, commodity and authority trust. And if not, not.

Probably not as catchy or as memorable, but definitely more trust-enhancing.

8

Network Trust and Federation

In a federation there is explicit encouragement of diversity and, dare we say it, subsidiarity, within an agreed overall framework. The central parts of the framework are there by peer agreement of the diverse parts, and the parts retain and develop their diversity by agreement of the centre. If that sounds a dynamic and possibly unstable place to be, well it often is.

When Ulrich Beck describes the impact of the Chernobyl nuclear accident on the German federation he points to the central place in the consciousness of the nation of fresh lettuce, now contaminated with radioactive poisons. Not only was there a full spectrum of expert opinion about the lettuces, from completely safe to eat, to fatally toxic, but according to the different official levels of 'safe' radioactivity in the different regions, the same lettuce was either acceptable or banned. This is not ultimately about better information, or more standardization and uniformity. It is about the way in which we interact in our beliefs about the world.

The real question would be why no one could imagine people's needs in the event of a nuclear accident before the event. Imagine the network trust needed to even raise such a question.

Businesses are to some extent federations and as we write we are watching Andersen go through the aftermath of the Enron scandal and a Federal investigation into the use of shredding to destroy evidence. Andersen people are protesting that it is unfair for the good work of the many to be trashed by the sharp practices of the few. Doubtless many Andersen people have striven to uphold standards of business best practice. It is also possible to make a case that no major audit company has consistently exposed poor practice in their clients, even when shareholders were at significant risk of severe losses.

So we are talking here about the way we deal with the opinions and views of others in a social world. We trust others to have thought through things we don't have time to think about or things they should have access to better information on. We also spot fashions and trends in opinion and make judgements about how much we want to run with the herd and how much we want to be different.

These two things interact. The euro currency is an exercise in federation and network trust. It removes certain state-oriented controls over the economy for the sake of an enforced common economic future. If you like, it means that the states in the euro zone have to negotiate aspects of their social and political programme in order to protect a common asset. Also as we write, the French presidential elections threw up a large vote for Le Pen who is against the euro in the sense that he would have liked to have retained the franc. However, if the franc had still been in place during this election, the vote for Le Pen would probably have caused a run on the franc and possibly driven it out of the exchange rate mechanism. So in a sense the euro enabled a protest vote to take place without major financial ramifications.

Pluralism, Inconsistency and Robustness

Network trust, more than any other in this book, is inconsistent. Not only do I trust, at some level, the views of my peers who do not agree with each other, but when someone's perspective fails me, I positively rely on being able to go to someone else for a perspective both on the original issue and on the failure. Diversity and pluralism are of the essence of network trust: if everyone thought the same about something, network trust would atrophy into authority trust or commodity trust in its search for consistency.

We need this inconsistency to provide robustness. It is the opposite of the hubris that knows all the answers. We find social and business paths by lots of people trying lots of different approaches. As we have said, authority trust and institutional nature grow whenever this is inappropriate or difficult to acknowledge publicly. We get robustness because there is always another place to turn to make progress, always another theory and always another set of relevant experiences. This book lives in that place of providing a wealth of other models and other perspectives for people to use when the conventional business approach lets them down.

Part of inconsistency is error. If we trust people around us we will be wrong much of the time. Of course from the perspective of network trust, the issue is whether we do better at predicting the things we need to predict, better at finding protection by the herd, better at learning how to work smarter next time than if we had failed to trust and gone our own solitary way.

Network trust is also about our basic needs for security, as Maslow described in his hierarchy of needs model of motivation. Until we have our basic needs for security and comfort met, we will not be engaging with issues of creativity and innovation, not looking for new ways to understand the world and our business. We typically find comfort and security in network trust, in the experience of people around us that this activity is safe (enough) and that the company is a trustworthy employer.

The Case of the Strange Business Model

My first employer, who in some ways is responsible for this book, had a business model that was successful at some unintended and subconscious level. It was a seismic contractor, operating oil exploration crews in exotic locations around the world, often in difficult conditions geographically, medically, socially and politically. A bunch of geophysicists with mechanics in support would get sent to some God-forsaken spot to acquire seismic data.

It appeared to those geophysicists thrown in at the deep end that the management decisions taken by head office were systematically barmy. For instance we would be working in irrigated farmland with heavy machinery that none of the bridges over the canals would support. Or classically at the behest of a major oil company we would start a survey with two crews a hundred miles apart and work towards a join based on three survey bases – satellite navigation data, a British imperial land survey and a local army survey.

The salvation was a recruitment policy that provided an endless stream of bright graduates, hungry for adventure and having endless resourcefulness and practical skills. The legend was, and the data supported this, that the further a crew was from head office, the more efficient it was. People worked with what they had, found ways to do what they had to do, had endless reasons for abandoning policy and instruction as the first move not the last. This could be alarming – driving the wrong way up slip roads in Benghazi or through armed checkpoints without stopping – this last on the grounds that the soldiers were not allowed ammunition.

The medium-term result of this situation was passable performance on contracts and a steady exodus of self-reliant and highly experienced graduates into safer oil company jobs. In this latter role they quickly became clients for the original, fondly remembered company, thus stabilizing the entire business model with a bizarre version of network trust.

In our experience it is rather common for the informal social system, based on network trust, to be stronger than the formal reporting structure and the official business processes. It can be very important to understand the real bases for action as against the way things are supposed to be done. We use a theatre metaphor for this, and talk about the difference between what happens on the stage and what happens backstage behind the scenes. It helps to understand that there has to be a backstage.

The Case of the Pub Back Door

We describe elsewhere the serial ritual slaughter of e-business exchanges. Here we take up another aspect of the case.

One of the operators (of pub restaurant chains) who was instrumental in funding the creation of an e-business exchange for purchasing food and other consumables in the foodservice sector turned out to have an interesting reason for doing so. The assumption that this was about automation and economic factors in the bulk purchase of food proved to be false.

If you imagine being a chef or manager in a pub restaurant you will feel the dynamism and service pressure typically felt – the large late-booked party, the sudden run on a certain sort of food, the crucial ingredients missing from today's order from the wholesaler. You can also imagine a steady stream of sales representatives pushing deals that do not necessarily accord with head-office buying policy. The policy is always to consolidate buying through preferred distributors and manufacturers to get economies of scale but also to assist in traceability when there is a food scare or a food poisoning complaint (or exceptionally even to recreate a curiously successful dish).

Now a restaurant is a cash economy, and it is impossible to overcome a tendency to 'back door' purchases where, almost literally, enterprising suppliers will come to the back door with something that the chef needs. The motivation for the e-business exchange was to channel more orders through a medium that was auditable both for financial and food safety reasons. Of course this motivation could not be part of the public face of the project – you don't talk openly about either your engagement with the black economy or about food suppliers who have never been audited.

In the pub example, the suppliers outside the system were closer to meeting the security and comfort needs of the chefs than were the official preferred suppliers. Network trust grew at the expense of authority trust because it was more effective at supporting getting the job done.

The Value of Words

One of the interesting findings of applying game theory to trust situations is that if a standard model of rational action is used, what people say does not make any difference to the situation. People have their preferences, and in a state of perfect knowledge the preferences of other people they know or like are already factored in. There is no room for verbal commitments, or promises, to change the situation at all.

> Words, words, mere words, no matter from the heart.
> *Troilus and Cressida*
> William Shakespeare (1564–1616)

We recognize this state of affairs from everyday organizational life of course. It is easy to have meetings and to make formal commitments that with hindsight did not change the course of events at all. It is not that people are insincere in their promises (though they may be), it is that given the set of entrenched interests in a situation, there is no room to implement the commitments made. In some way what is said is not systemic, does not reflect the way things work.

It is even easier to recognize this effect when institutions make pronouncements, for instance about public safety:

> During the BSE crisis in the UK, various government departments and ministers made statements about the safety of British beef. These statements had already been discounted by the public and all the protestations of scientific evidence and due process only made the public more distrustful of what they were being told.
>
> As perceptions grew that the probability of terrorist outrages was on the increase as UN weapons inspection deadlines approached in Iraq, the UK government was torn between communicating its intelligence to the general public and the risk of causing panic through being misunderstood in some way. No effective and trusted communication channel existed. Those from wartime had long since atrophied and no new ones had since been put in place.

There are several problems with the communications model that institutions use in these situations:

(1) They have a model of knowledge that can be possessed by them and transmitted to the people who they think need to know.

(Actually difficult communications always need shared understanding and two-way communication.)

(2) They think that they will be trusted because they are good and
knowledgeable chaps who are there to protect the public interest.
(Actually whether they are acting in the public interest is not
theirs to judge.)

(3) They think they have to defend against ideas and data that did
not originate with them because they cannot control them.
(Actually their ability to embrace external expertise and ideas is
a key indicator for judgements about trustworthiness.)

(4) Although they may be able to recognize public hysteria, they do
not have any insight into how to deal with it effectively. (They
do not and cannot take responsibility for the strategic effects of
their pronouncements.)

There is always a muddle between trusting the institution and trusting its advice. They are not the same thing. If the institution is not
already trusted – perhaps because it is new, for example – then its
pronouncements will be treated sceptically. If it has to deal with a
crisis early in its lifetime it is unlikely to be effective. If an institution is trusted then its pronouncements may be heard unless it is
obviously under external pressure. A government department
cannot be trusted when the government's reputation is at stake from
its actions because it is highly unlikely to be able to act as it sees
fit. People know how to discount what they are told in certain circumstances.

The authoritativeness of an institution's pronouncements is
double-edged. When people are projecting leadership onto an institution it is expected to make clear and unequivocal statements. Much
of the debate about statistical illiteracy and people's ability to interpret statements about risk actually revolves around the need for
leadership, rather than the request for information. However, authoritativeness can also be interpreted as isolation and arrogance. Indeed,
some people will interpret an institution's stance in one way and
some in the other. This is only to say that people's needs in the
messages that are given out are very different (treat me as I am, not
as you want me to be).

It makes more sense to think of testing the ability of an organization to get important and difficult messages across should the need

arise. Before a high-stress situation arises it is possible to actively promote trust and a sense of service. On this basis it is possible to get information across and to deal with people's needs for advice – but it only makes sense to assess this before the need arises, and the only actions that can be effective need to take place before the need arises.

> Never trust a bloke who says 'trust me'.
>> Advice from a young woman who knows

The thinking that says that we will find out in due course whether an institution is effective is actually abusive of the public, who will not be able to engage when their need arises.

PART 3

Introduction to Authority Trust

Propositions to be forbidden:

that the sun is immovable at the centre of the heaven;

that the earth is not at the centre of the heaven, and is not immovable, but moves by a double motion.

> Holy Office of the Inquisition, Codex
> 1181 Proceedings against Galileo
> Galilei, Rome, February 1616

Authority trust is the power that enables hierarchies to impose constraints on people within them. Its power derives from a centralized decision-making process and the fear of sanction attached to non-compliance. In social or political terms its influence runs from anarchy at one extreme, where authority trust is low or non-existent, to totalitarianism at the other, where it is high and all-pervading, where choices are completely constrained to those options that fall within the prescribed limits. Spread between these two extremes are all the many hierarchies that modern life runs on and of which we are all, in our business, social and economic activities, participants at some level. As decision making becomes more centralized it

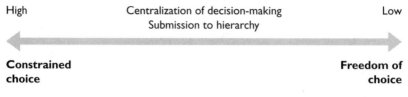

Figure P3.1

becomes necessary to trust the decision-making authority more and over a wider range of issues. People often welcome the restriction of choice as it relieves their responsibility for the effects of the choices they make. In close up, the dimensions of authority trust in our model are as shown in Figure P3.1.

Deriving Authority Trust

There are a number of institutions that have a self-defined and self-consistent view of the world. They are founded on the belief that there is a single reality that can be mediated by the institution. This is sometimes described as a unitary worldview. For these institutions it does not make sense to describe an alternative perspective.

Take, for instance, the UK legal system (although most legal systems share the characteristics we are interested in). The job of the legal system is to understand whether or not people brought before the courts have or have not broken laws. There may be imperfections in the process of deciding on guilt or innocence, but the system has a consistent internal definition of that guilt or innocence, and a consistent view of its own task.

It is common for such systems to defend themselves from challenges to their authority by being able to hand down punishments for disrespect. The crime here is to question whether the court has the ability to make a judgement that meets common sense views of justice as well as the unitary internal view. The crime transcends mere disrespect and becomes contempt, a far more potent charge. You can clearly see the unitary view of the system in its insistence that the common sense view has no basis or legitimacy, and its need to suppress such judgements.

Just imagine for a moment having two legal systems with two different (but reasonable) sets of laws. There would doubtless be a significant set of people who would be innocent under one system and guilty under another. Imagine the position of the police, the courts and the public as consumers of justice. But in a way this would be a rational and reasonable system, enabling people to understand the degree to which judgements of guilt and innocence were actually marginal and contingent.

Trust in Unitary Worlds

Unitary systems demand trust in their worldview, in their authoritative statements about how things are. If a court says someone is guilty then he is, possibly pending the deliberations of various review systems. When those judged guilty, and their supporters, proclaim and maintain their innocence, then the system closes ranks to reject their claim. It has very specific procedures for allowing official re-examination of the case. The rest of the world is supposed to trust the system to deliver justice.

> When it comes to the creation of saints, the Roman Catholic Church – about as unitary an authority as there is – has something of a monopoly. It is important for the church's authority that the faithful trust the process that delivers them saints.
>
> The role of Promoter of the Faith – better known to us as the Devil's Advocate – was created in 1587 to exclude saintly candidates against whom evidence could be found that their deaths were not proved to be 'precious in the sight of God'. No part of the process by which we get new saints is valid without the presence and full concurrence of the Devil's Advocate.

There is no other position available. You cannot say that the legal system has its good days and its bad days. You cannot say that it works well for certain sorts of cases but not for others, if by that you mean that you do not accept its jurisdiction over the parts where it does not perform well. Basically, you either trust the system or you don't, and the difficulty with not trusting is finding a viable alternative institution. When you have a need to resort to the legal system, not only you but also the other parties involved must accept, or be coerced into accepting, the judgement of the courts.

There are, of course, legal systems where the tension between legal justice and some more grounded view of justice is only too plain. When courts fall under the sway of governments or of organized crime then people understand that the unitary claim of a single reality is flawed. In extreme cases such as the paramilitary organizations in Northern Ireland, there are parallel legal systems that hold sway in their own constituencies.

For another example, think of rail safety. There is much detailed legislation that describes what safety is and how it is to be achieved. The rail authorities have safety cases for what they do and detailed procedures for operation and maintenance of tracks, trackside equipment and trains. In the course of normal operation many things happen that are, on the face of it, dangerous and risky to the public. We are well aware of SPADs (Signals Passed At Danger), but there are also right-side and wrong-side failures, where trains get to be in places they shouldn't be, either following or head-on to other trains. Within the unitary view of rail safety; these things are entirely accounted for and there are procedures for investigating and dealing with them.

After a major accident, there is another point of view briefly available to the enquiry set up. The other perspective is that the unitary, internally consistent view of safety dealt with by systems and procedures is not actually consistent with the possibilities of keeping passengers from harm. Very often, the discomfort about the possibility that the way the safety system works may not be in the interest of passengers gets diverted into arguments about technology choices and investment, or into arguments about industry structure and accountability. In authority trust structures, nobody wants to tangle with the basic question about whether the institution is acting in the public interest, whether its view of the world is consistent with the needs of the people it is there to serve.

The Leadership Question

The leadership question appears as a question about the trust of followers. In unitary systems everything is a leadership question, because the system can only change from within, from the top of the hierarchy. As soon as there is a challenge that implies more than one possible reality then the system cannot generate authority trust. If an external agency improves rail safety, then the official providers of rail safety are brought into disrepute.

Followers have a more plural world than the institution in question because they live in and with several important institutions. Only fascist political systems attempt to reconcile all institutions. Leadership is about including enough of the other realities that followers live with to allow or impose authority trust. They have to arrange that the credibility question *does not arise*. Leadership must already have dealt with the questions and issues that may arise for followers. In this sense the leadership must pay attention to other realities than the one it generates, giving a strange contradiction in the heart of the system.

In general these unitary systems consume their energy putting out their message and managing news and perceptions. They become unable to listen to other realities at the level they need to and they drift out of touch with the other realities of their followers. This dynamic leads to a crumbling of authority trust. If power and force of character are used to maintain the trust, then it will fail suddenly when the tension between it and other realities becomes too great.

Authority trust is consistent, as we have seen. When it becomes unavailable its hierarchy fragments into network trust as people scramble for safety and things becomes inconsistent. The medieval church provides us with another classic example of the effect of there suddenly being more than one possible reality. In Europe until the Reformation in the sixteenth century there had been only one church, one authority and one commodity – Christianity. Afterwards there would always be at least two – Catholicism and Protestantism. In an effort to regain its ascendancy and restore its reputation, Rome, in 1662, created its institution for the propagation of the faith. Its work over the centuries has been commodified for us by the derived term 'propaganda'.

Sometimes leadership becomes synonymous with an abstract concept as in the case of Enron and the concept of creative destruction.

In this case a policy is made to appear a success at all costs, because the company is actually floating on the hype of invincibility surrounding the concept. Again, there is no mechanism for the resolution of this reality with other important realities.

One vital question for leadership seems paradoxical: how do you learn to be a leader? It would seem that the best leaders had their years of sackcloth and ashes when their ideas could find no real resonance and opportunity, before somehow coming to power. Learning to lead may include learning to deal with the other realities because you must before coming to power when the force of that 'must' is reduced.

Whistle Blowing

We see these issues most clearly in business organizations when there are cases of whistle blowing. Where an individual becomes convinced that the actions of a company that employs him are against the public interest he may go public with damaging revelations. Notice that this is a tension between the official position of the company (a unitary reality, interpreted for all by the company management) and the citizen reality of the whistle blower.

It is a measure of the degree of authority trust expected in the business world that the fate of whistle blowers is uniformly poor. No one wants to employ someone who will put citizenship ahead of loyalty to employer. By doing so they would have to acknowledge that all their employees have potentially divergent realities from the company reality.

Is there a model for success for whistle blowers? In the political world, Nelson Mandela, who stood publicly for another reality than the official government position and eventually came to symbolize and then to enact that other reality, shows that the tide can change. Interestingly, in that case there was a change from a rather unitary and authoritarian government to a more plural model.

There are, of course, many more open and inclusive company cultures where the question of whistle blowing would not arise.

The Risk of Authority Trust

As with the case of Enron already mentioned, to use a system of authority trust is to put all your eggs in one basket. When the system fails you will probably lose the whole system, no matter how big or powerful it appears to be. By effectively ironing out all the smaller wrinkles and imposing a consistent view of the world, all the information that might point to smaller risks that need paying attention to is lost.

9

The Crucial Link between Authority Trust and Business Risk

The most intractable business risks are, of course, those that we unwittingly create. As we have seen, authority trust generates both business risk directly and barriers to addressing business risk. The problems are caused by:

- the growth of a systemic blindness to the way other people think;
- the growth of instincts about solutions that are systematically misleading;
- progressive damage to relationships with customers.

Problems that are caused by misguided investment will never be seen as problems: they are supposed to be solutions and will be perceived as such. This is the root of why people, when they are failing to solve a problem, often try more of the solution that just made things worse.

The Case of the Wrong Solution
A colleague worked for a large military contractor as a professional risk manager. The key business risks stemmed from performance issues around cost and delivery times. These were putting pressure on all sorts of other areas. The problem was being addressed by the

investment of £15 m in the integrated project support environment – a bureaucratic and technical support structure to avoid the worst mistakes made in software development. Software development was and is a major source of performance problems. The risk manager looked at the issues and did a systematic study on performance issues. He found that the productivity gap between the best and the average software developer was a factor of twenty (this is not news). Since we are talking here about thousands of programmers and potential recruits, his view was that a very modest investment in HR to provide a better working environment and more successful recruitment of key individuals would give a much better financial return and come closer to addressing the business risk. The figures were bullet proof. Although this colleague caught the twinkle in the MD's eye, this solution was not available, and, indeed, there were (only partly tongue in cheek) warnings about car parks and dark nights. The integrated support environment directly builds authority trust – finding and developing key staff demands that authority trust be kept in check.

We see in this case study a typical predilection for investment in process, procedure, equipment and technique. These things are sold as supporting work but actually communicate distrust and a desire to become less dependent on skills and judgement. No one models the large-scale and long-term implications for social relationships of these types of investment.

The Shadow Side of Process

The concept of the shadow side insists that for everything that is positive, explicit and goal oriented, there is a set of negative, unac-knowledged and subconsciously driven factors that mirror and balance them. Like a shadow, the shadow side is part of the way things are that we just have to live with. It is the shadow side that results in hubris getting its come-uppance and overweening power being humbled. To be in touch with the shadow side, you have to be at peace with yourself.

A good process is a wonderful and enabling thing. Deming believed that 85% of performance could be attributed to process and that looking for individual responsibility for outcomes was largely pointless. Where people both understand this and are well intentioned, then work on the process is construed as support for colleagues, and managers can find a mode of 'servant leadership' that brings out the best in people.

But a process that is supposed to compensate for the deficits of the people pushes energy into the shadow side. The contradiction between the proposition that the process is supposed to be an improvement and support and the attitude of mistrust and devaluation results in ambivalence between management and process users and between users and the process. There will be shadow processes which people use to get their own work goals met, and these shadow processes will conflict with and subvert the official process. When trying to improve the official process, there will be a constant tension between how things are supposed to work and how they work in practice. Many improvements that ought to work on a logical argument end up making things worse.

People need trust in order to do work. Managers need trust in order to manage. The trust that people need is often systematically excluded in favour of authority trust: in effect, there is no way for a worker to be independently right, insightful or valuable in what he or she does. The worker is no longer human in trust terms. Sometimes this is explicitly repressive. More often it stems from the growth of authority trust itself, that the only thing that really counts is management's view of the job to be done and the official process and modes of organizing. Each new crisis and difficulty only tightens the screw: nothing can reverse the process of centralization of trust.

The Customer Is Always Right

This same statement 'the customer is always right' is used to justify everything from complete trust of the customer to complete distrust. From the standpoint of authority trust we can see that this is a useful diagnostic because there is no reason for the customer to have authority trust.

The Case of the Dodgy Diamond

A colleague visited a number of organizations in the USA which had reputations for outstanding customer service. One of these had a well-established policy of giving a full, no-questions-asked returns policy on goods it sold. The policy was a cornerstone of its reputation for service. The organization had recently diversified into selling jewellery. One of its sales staff was put on the spot by a customer returning a diamond ring worth $4000. The salesperson was un-comfortable because of the possibility that the stone in the ring had been swapped for a fake but had no way of telling. Unwilling to take responsibility herself, she called the owner of the company for instructions. The answer, or we would not be telling the story, was two-fold:

- Whatever you choose to do is right because we trust our staff.
- Our policy is clear and if we have not thought it through that is our problem.

There are plenty of organizations where the customer is the subject of deep mistrust and of constant belittling. That does not mean that the customer is not also kow-towed to. The combination of these is quite a common pattern. The implication is, of course, that we in our institutionalized hierarchic trust know what the customer needs (or can be persuaded to buy) better than the customer does himself, and that there is nothing of the customer's perspective we need to understand except to manage or change it.

To trust customers is to make it clear that the relationship is in some sense unconditional. How many times have you had a conversation with an organization that seemed warm and sincere while you were in play, but turned cold and dismissive as soon as there was no longer a deal on the table? This makes business-as-we-know-it sense but no sense at all if customers and potential customers are to be people with their own separate, valid and independent way of being. It is, of course, the potential customers who are *not* won who hold the secret of extending the market.

A Product that Shows Mistrust of Customers

We are all aware now of the deal you get buying an inkjet printer – low initial cost and very high consumables cost. Manufacturers go to increasing lengths to make sure that you have to buy only their consumables so they get to meet their vision of the business deal. I recently came across a data projector at a price of around £500 – real breakthrough. The deal, however, is that a new bulb costs £300. After a thousand hours of use the unit closes itself down and has to be returned to the manufacturer: it proved beyond a highly skilled engineer to even get near the bulb enclosure.

Control Behaviour and Business Risk

The Peter principle says that you will be promoted to the level of your incompetence. We want to take that analysis one step further. What happens when people feel out of their depth is that they move to trying to control events such that their incompetence will not be exposed. Their actions become defensive in the sense that there are certain situations that they cannot allow to arise. Rare indeed is the individual or the culture that can allow lack of control to be seen and loss of face to happen, content that the only way to learn is to make mistakes.

Business risk is under-acknowledged and under-reported because the people who need to deal with it are uncomfortable being seen to manage it (or to mismanage it). Much business risk is new in the sense that it has not occurred before. You can therefore never have a track record that indicates that you might be competent in dealing with the risks to come. And maybe the only thing that is worse than being seen not to manage risk effectively is having some young Turk or unproven outsider show you how to do it.

One of the least attractive sides of business as we know it is its conservatism in selecting staff. We go to huge lengths to define capabilities and psychological profile, demand that people have been successful in a similar job recently, even headhunt successful people from our rivals, and end up pursuing the same failing solution that we are already addicted to. What else could possibly happen?

Psychologically, when people are under pressure they regress to the last time they were successful.

So business risk is precisely the challenge that the business has not met before and yet the notion that a new scenario and a new era might demand different behaviour is beyond us. Why, precisely because of authority trust. The organization as institution must have an answer. We cannot tolerate the uncertainty and ambiguity of being in an institution that cannot protect us. We may well be in such an institution, but we cannot acknowledge it. Maybe as we see mighty organizations brought low on a regular basis we will learn to behave differently, but our analysis here is that it is precisely the defensive cast of mind brought about by being required to be in control when this is not reasonable or even possible that drives the growth of authority trust and thus compounds the problem. There is no situation when trust is more crucial than when facing a risk that can seriously damage the business. Authority trust is precisely the wrong sort of trust in this situation because it does not support. Its illusory, fantasy nature becomes most exposed precisely when it is needed to address reality.

The Case of Serial Ritual Slaughter

In the UK as in many countries there are two supply chains in the food sector: the retail supply chain to supermarkets and shops and the foodservice supply chain to hotels and restaurants as well as public sector providers such as schools and prisons. In the retail sector the commercial might of the supermarket majors has kicked reform into the supply chain and it has a high level of automation. The foodservice sector is the poor cousin, using primitive methods and casting anxious looks over its shoulders in case more efficient players want to take its market away. Throughout the whole food sector standards of business behaviour are very low, with bullying, dirty tricks and broken agreements the norm rather than the exception.

As part of the negotiated reform of the foodservice sector there were cabals formed to see if new technology, including automation and e-business exchanges, could be deployed. Interestingly, the industry split horizontally rather than vertically. The 'operators' – the big hotel and pub chains – would rather collaborate with each other, although

nominally in direct competition, than with distributors and manufacturers to give an integrated supply chain. So the operators formed
a club, poured money into the creation of an e-business exchange,
committed to the formation of a separate company to run the
exchange so that it could be neutral, and then turned to the rest of
the sector to see if they would play.

In the meantime the distributors were worried. They were already,
in their own eyes, over a barrel with regard to their margins. They
could not allow an exchange to be developed that would fix prices
directly between the manufacturers and the operators. So they met
in a smoke-filled room and the thumbs went down. The operators'
exchange was dead and their money lost. Of course the issue of
reform was still on the table and who better to take it up than the
distributors. They duly committed to building an exchange and went
to sign up the manufacturers to using it.

The manufacturers were already fed up with the demands for
supply chain integration from the supermarkets, which had at least as
much of an eye to excluding their rivals as to genuine moves to develop
efficiency. They duly turned down what would have amounted to just
another set of demands from the distributors – many manufactures supply both retail and foodservice. And as we write this it is quite likely that
the manufacturers may have their own go at developing an exchange.

We can see in the case study immense expenditure of effort and
energy without ever dealing with the fundamentals of business risk.
This is not restricted to the senior managers involved: the big five
consultants brought in to do the business case for the operators were
equally blind. These people all know each other well, but in a climate
of mistrust and public humiliation, when one is outsmarted the
chances of addressing the business fundamentals are tiny. Note that
in this business no one trusts their customers.

Trust Dynamics

In the preceding sections we have outlined several ways in which
authority trust is reinforced. There is a sort of entropy that pushes

towards increasing authority trust, which generally means reduced authentic trust and network trust. Bad money, if you like, drives out good. This drift cannot be reversed without taking personal risk. No change programme ever built authentic and network trust without people taking on themselves the risk of sticking their necks out and trusting others because they wanted to and to build a better culture.

But equally, from any place on the map of trust, from any organizational culture, there is generally a better place towards authentic and network trust. If you want to harness people's ability, energy and commitment, if you want to perform better at dealing with new risks and new opportunities, then dismantle some authority trust and make sure no one gets shot when they take personal risks. It is fundamentally the way our culture punishes the taking of personal risk that drives trust to that authority place. In the end you either trust people to do the job or you trust the installed business processes and management direction of them. People see very quickly which of those things is really valued and where the money and management time is spent.

Reforming Authority Trust

Some readers will remember the beginnings of the end of Soviet communism when the order went out from Gorbachev to start bottom-up reforms called *perestroika*. The world did a double-take – how could you give top-down orders to repressed party officials to start thinking for themselves?

We need to take this conundrum seriously wherever authority trust is a major part of the existing situation. If we return to the example of the UK construction industry we looked at in the introduction, we can see the issues. There are people in the industry who know how to get far better commercial outcomes by increasing the level of trust between parties in the supply chain. However:

- The government does not fund them to a realistic level even though it is government policy to do so. Although the research and pilot project results are compelling, the major players in the industry have not moved. The industry authority is voting in a different direction and actually the government is more sensitive to the power of these major players than it is to its own objectives.

- The clients for the major projects that would benefit from reform know that huge savings are available, but try to access those savings by putting commercial pressure on the main contractors. They appear to believe that it is not their behaviour that has to change and that sooner or later their contractors will get their act together. In the meantime, they do not want to risk things getting worse before they get better: they are after short-term comfort on the current project. Immediate concerns dominate everything.
- The main contractors feel that they are in a position to be squeezed by their client on one side and their supply chain on the other. If they are not tough they will go to the wall. They, more than anyone, know what can be achieved but they feel they cannot access it until conditions become easier.
- The sub-contractors feel that any suggestion they make is treated as a plea for special treatment and raises suspicion of their motives. In any case it is not down to them to show leadership in a situation where the power players have turned their back on better outcomes.

Authority trust is just that. It concentrates policy and leadership at the top of a hierarchy and the authority defines what the way forward is. When someone else says, 'there is a better way forward over here' they create a discordance because it cannot be better while authority is defining the way forward. Other agencies, such as governments which have a similar authority trust style, are very unwilling to undermine existing authority as by doing so people may well draw parallels with the need to reform the government's own use of power and trust.

Ways Forward

We know that when things are stuck, there is always a better way – it's to the north-east of our current position on the trust map. This means more network trust and more authentic trust to counterbalance the overemphasis on authority trust and commodity trust. So the emphasis on process and service levels must be relaxed at the same time as the leadership starts to generate more space for people to contribute from their own resources: let a thousand flowers grow.

This is precisely what has been done, for instance, in the supply chain for building Sainsbury stores. Long-term collaboration is exercised over many projects, a form of information exchange and collaboration around the construction process that allows and encourages contribution and innovation. Interestingly, for Sainsbury this is a competitive advantage, allowing it to open new stores in a quarter of the time it used to take, and it does not particularly want to give that advantage away.

To give an idea just how simple and practical these moves can be, one of the things done with the information system that links the supply chain on these projects is to publish photographs of the site! These photos are regularly updated to show progress and allow suppliers to see what is going on without having to visit. This saves costs all round, reduces site congestion and triggers actions that would otherwise be missed. Such general gains are just not on the agenda when people are focused on doing what they have been asked to do in the way they have been asked to do it.

Changing Data

It is a truism that you get what you measure. If a manager's belief is that his workers and suppliers are basically irresponsible, he will put management practices in place that amply show that irresponsibility is widespread and that the practices need to be strengthened. Where the opposite beliefs are implemented we get high-powered teams and exceptional results, but these are not transferable because from the first perspective there are obviously special factors or just luck at work there. And because our minds are wonderfully subtle things we should be aware of a tendency to believe one thing while professing to believe another. I can cheerfully profess my trust in such a way that people know instinctively that a trap is being set.

The heart of what forms the belief that managers have of the situation and the control they need to have in order to manage it is the promotion system for managers. Our deepest beliefs about work are revealed in the way we promote people who are politically astute, who have that determination and can-do attitude, who are ambitious and amoral. But of course these people, while they are effective in the authority trust system, are the very last people who will allow other ways of working to develop. They know instinctively and they have been rewarded for thinking that they need to exert authority and control to maintain the effectiveness of the system. (When did people ever get promoted by being open, honest and able to bring out the best in others?)

Part of the reason we think this way is the 'islands of sanity' argument. To have an island of trust is to invite it to be subverted by more cynical people alongside it. That is what such people do. However, if trust is authentic and internally motivated for its own sake, then it can cope with such attacks so long as they are not used to demonstrate in the wider system that trust does not work. Areas of trust do not need special privileges but neither do they need to be destroyed by spurious political arguments.

10

A Case Study in Authority Trust and Institutions: When POSIWIDs Collide

Note to readers: the following essay contains extensive and scary reification: extensive because authority trust and institutions are impossible – cannot exist – without it and scary because they reify us for precisely the same reasons. As a trust-building rule of thumb, the more reification you can point to, the more inauthentic publicness is demanded from the players involved.

In the end it is not possible to talk about trust without mentioning doctors. Somehow everything gets wrapped up in how we share responsibility for our health with highly trained medical professionals. Since we want to transfer the understanding to the world of business, let's use the following mapping:

- The medical profession is an institution: it has its own values, its own tribal loyalty, its own governance – likewise Tesco, IBM, Railtrack, British Airways, the XYZ Widget Co. etc.
- The relevant local body, perhaps the doctor's surgery, perhaps the local NHS Trust, is also an institution. In some matters the primary loyalty is to the employing institution rather than the professional body – your local branch, your BA flight.

- The doctor is the immediate interface for a patient. The doctor is the concrete face of the institutions as far as the patient is concerned. Likewise the staff at the local branch, your BA crew.
- The patient is the service user. The patient may not think in terms of the institution, only in terms of the doctor and the service parameters, such as how long it takes to get an appointment (we show later that when, for example, as shoppers, our view of service use and the institution's view are not aligned, the institutions attempt to bridge the gap or cover the difference by means of an authority trust relationship).

For our concerns here the crucial step is 'going to the doctor'. In taking the step of consulting a medical professional we medicalize the problem. If the medical paradigm is inappropriate for our presenting problem, whatever it might be, then we run a grave risk of being pulled into a system and its set of judgements from which there is no real escape. We are trapped because we have no way of asserting our internal judgements against the weight of medical expertise and the institutional power of the profession.

This is what institutions do. It is no criticism of the medical profession or any other institution to say that it brings the power of its view of the world to bear on the people who interact with it. For good or for ill, in engaging with an institution that is what you get.

Let's briefly look at the other end of the pipeline. Many people feel after the event that the service they have had from a doctor is deficient in some way. They would like to feel that their concerns about the service are recognized, both for their own sake and for the sake of other users. Usually the practical form of this is to complain to the doctor or the surgery and to expect an apology. However, this is not the nature of the relationship or the nature of institutions. The doctor, having failed to apologize, the complaint goes into a formal procedure and investigations are carried out. Escalation is common as the patient who complained begins to feel that the system is defensive and is not prepared to simply acknowledge that things could have been better. The cost in money and relationship terms of this behaviour is huge – the basic apology was essentially cost free and there is an escalation of cost and aggravation of approximately ten-fold at each escalation step. When it comes to the real interaction between the institution and its users, we are not in a sensible or pragmatic world. Attempts to address these issues regularly fail.

The patient attempts to treat the doctor as a person and as a friend. The pattern is very different when a consultation is mediated in other ways. The doctor, however, puts his trust not in the patient relationship but in the institution. Indeed, the private abuse of the relationship in the enciphered notes a doctor makes is legendary. Although the doctor may be critical of what goes on in a practice or a hospital, actually there is no possibility of practice outside the institution, and the values and norms of the institution are the daily stuff of a doctor's life.

Some of what the institution stands for is important – research and the establishment of standards in training and the ability to discipline and exclude practitioners who go beyond the pale in some way. Much of what consumes the institution is at least in touch with patient priorities, though that sense of political possibility cannot be explicit because of the explicit primacy of clinical judgement. But if we take the opposite extreme, the medical profession, certainly in the UK, insists on a complete separation between bodily and mental disease. No thinking doctor would support this as a patient-centred distinction: rare is the body disease that does not affect the mind and rarer the mental affliction that does not affect the body. Neither diagnosis nor treatment is well served by the distinction. But the provision of service is institutionalized and there is no realistic prospect of integration. If you see your GP he can send you to see a mental specialist or one of a range of specialists in aspects of bodily dysfunction.

The role the institution plays as an institution is to consolidate and underpin medical practice. If we said that the purpose of the system (POSIWID) was to provide careers for doctors and to enshrine the pecking order of health professionals, we would not miss the mark by far. So the presenting problem of a patient is a medical issue: nothing else has an institutional response. (Since they have to deal with other institutions, all institutions are forever Janus-like. In fact in many cases they are hydra-headed. The more views they must take, the more constrained become their service offerings. Doctors, for example, exist within the institution of the NHS whose POSIWID, it can be argued, is to employ loads of people, provide channels to market for drug companies and consume political energy and resources through attention-grabbing headlines.)

Now, there have been excellent studies into ways of increasing the quality of the relationship between patient and doctor. One treats the institution as a machine and asks how the patient can get organized to maximize the quality and effectiveness of the response that machine provides. The second forms focus groups to explicitly set local spending priorities to override the institutional mechanisms. We can generalize these studies to say that in confronting an institution and its default authority trust system, we can either change ourselves to get the best outcome available to us short of changing the institution, or we can organize with others in a similar position to grab the levers of power in some way. What we cannot do is to expect authority trust systems to take cognisance of the different world we live in and the different values we may have. That is not what institutions do.

The Case of NHS Direct

NHS Direct provides a phone-in service to give medical advice and to refer callers to appropriate medical treatment. Tellingly, although it is a local service provided by local staff, one of the political aims for the service is to standardize service across the country. To do this the nurses who staff the call centres use a standard decision support system to guide them through a standard series of questions to arrive at a treatment option.

My first question was then 'have you noticed that certain callers have learned how to get the response they want out of the system by answering the questions in a certain way?' The answer was immediate: people had learned how to play the system almost as soon as it was rolled out. This was not thought to be a particular problem. (In another context, this point illustrates perfectly the argument put forward by the police (one of our truly great institutions) that slick lawyers (another) have learned how to play the courts (another) in order to secure acquittals for defendants that the police 'know' to be guilty. Colliding POSIWIDS find it impossible to focus on service delivery. In fact, it's probably the last thing they have in mind.)

So the issue in dealing with an institution is that the frame of reference for the institution is a given – you can only deal with it on its own terms. As a trust issue this is huge. Our working definition of trust is that the person (or institution) that we trust will look after our interests. But our interests may well not be part of the frame of the institution and cannot even be seen by the institution. This is the nature of authority trust. By its nature it only deals with what it deals with and it cannot put its own concerns on one side in order to learn a different view of the world from someone else. Authority trust is consistent, it cannot be contingent or provisional in that way. To learn a different perspective would be to split the world and be left with an irreconcilable tension.

We should not underestimate the violence of such a tension. Ulrich Beck describes how in Germany in the immediate aftermath of Chernobyl, people who were used to taking extreme care of their health and who knew how to choose the very best fresh foods were suddenly in a position where fresh food was likely to be highly radioactive. They could not trust their eyes or other senses; the media were full of the most contradictory advice. There was nowhere to turn. Growers could not sell a lettuce no matter what. People's internal worlds were suddenly torn apart. If you listen to the stories of people who have been severely let down by the health service, they have this character of disorientation and almost psychotic distress.

Institutions from the Inside

As a member (as distinct from an inmate) of an institution trying to provide a service, the issues raised above are very difficult. They stem from the institution's inability to trust its members to do their individual thing to the greater glory of the institution. This inability to trust can have very real roots, as we shall see.

Since we have done doctors, we may as well do the police. The point of service access for a member of the public using the police service is often a crisis. We have been robbed, involved in a car accident, come on the scene of a violent crime. Our day-to-day concerns and interests are already disrupted and torn, and we need a speedy intervention. The point of the service provided by the police is to re-stabilize the situation and provide some immediate redress, not to deal with the wider context and the subtleties of what went on. Our need to have our interests looked after is dominated by the immediacy of the situation, not by our individuality and different perspective on the world.

A Road Accident in Nigeria

To illustrate how the police service might be different in a different culture with different needs, let me recount a story from Nigeria twenty years ago. I was working with a large team of local people doing oil exploration in the bush. One day as I accompanied a supervisor to see the work, we met all the workers returning to base. One of their number had had a road accident and it is unlucky to work on such a day. I expected to go and see the situation of the accident but was warned to stay away for fear of reprisal. After two hours we went to see the scene of the accident. Police rules were to impound the vehicles and take the drivers to the police station. The policeman at the scene told us where to bail the driver that evening. (This is only relevant in a western context, but our driver had clearly attempted an emergency stop to avoid a car doing a U-turn across the central reservation of a dual carriageway road.) Much to my amazement, the driver gave me his wages and asked me to find his family to give them to. Owing to another dispute no one bailed the driver that evening and by the next day it was impossible to release him from custody.

In the rough and ready situation of an emergency we have a more rough and ready perspective on trust. Our basic deal with the police is that they do stabilize a situation and not make it worse. As an institution the police have to deliver a service that is not highly sensitive to local needs but is robust and effective against the power of people operating outside the law. On occasion, this institutional culture gets them into the crossfire between social groups and they can be seen to fail on a massive scale by provoking riots – the very opposite of stabilization.

It is possible to have an open and liberal institution that trusts its members to contribute to its goals. Some membership organizations have this character. Authority (hierarchic) trust, the trust that one's superiors know better, is incompatible with that trust. Now for the police the pressure they are under leads to a need for hierarchic trust. The days of the 'bobby on the beat' are over not just because of efficiency drives and panda cars but because the relative isolation that allowed the village policeman to do his job to the best of his ability, for good or ill, have been blown away by communication and organization on both the side of the police force and the world of crime.

Building Trust in Institutions

From our perspective, building trust in an institution is a most paradoxical activity. An institution grows up to deliver a service or to colonize some particular part of the social ground. It thrives or not according to whether it can command resources in doing what it does. The concept of paying attention to service provision and to the perspectives of service consumers is foreign to the notion of building an institution. An institution finds for itself what the optimum parameters for service provision are in a way that is independent of the perspectives of its consumers. Religious institutions are perhaps the exemplar of this, but we have seen sports governing bodies provide excellent examples as well.

So if an institution perceives itself to have lost the trust of its consumers we have the strange concept of trying to find an alternative self-definition for the institution that will command trust. And of course trust is not there for the commanding. Once an institution is seen not to be in the general interest of society or the constituency it serves, then reinvention is problematic. What tends to happen is that the public, who by definition the institution does not understand, are harangued about what the 'real' issues are. The idea that some adjustment, change of procedure or trimming of the sails could be performed to improve levels of trust misses the point entirely.

Indeed, when an institution comes under pressure to perform differently or just more efficiently, it can only fall back on its authority trust, which will cause it to close ranks around its own concept of the world. Think of teachers being given lessons by government ministers in how to teach. The trust issue is framed by the government as one of trustworthiness – can we trust these professionals to do the best for our children? But the institution of teaching exists to understand precisely that question on behalf of the rest of society. The pressure leads to a more closed attitude and quite possibly to worse results. We could also talk about the externalization of the issue into one of marks and exam scores, a process which does more fundamental damage to education and to trust in the profession.

The Case of Value Baked Beans

Supermarkets by their nature compete on price, among other things. But sheer price competition can damage profits, so they invented a new ploy. The proposition is that you get what you pay for. If too many people are buying the cheapest brand and shopping around even for that then they clearly, from a supermarket point of view, have not understood that the supermarket understands value better than they do: it is the supermarket's institutional purpose to put forward the shopping choices that people need. So what happened was the introduction of a Value range (by that name or some similar) in very distinctive and unattractive packaging and with an unpleasant formulation inside. Some of these products are so bad that major suppliers refused to supply them, fearful for their reputation. Of course, people, especially the poor and vulnerable, cannot be seen in public buying trash, so the range forces people to move upmarket in the purchasing. The supermarkets can brag about how cheap their food is while raking in profit from people who cannot afford what they are forced/persuaded to buy.

So in business, authority trust can develop because of the pressure of the market, because of ambition to define the market, because of regulation or because of stiff competition. Any sort of pressure may force a business back on a centralized and hierarchically defined view of the world where people have to trust their boss and ultimately the institution as a whole. This systematically destroys authentic trust and the ability to deploy real degrees of freedom.

What we notice is that incipient authority trust generates all the wrong reactions. People centralize in an attempt to create trustworthiness when they should be decentralizing to give scope for the development of authentic trust. People attempt to make others more trustworthy, compounding two mistakes in one move: one – it's never about trustworthiness, and two – doing things to other people is no substitute for sorting out how we ourselves need to change.

PART 4

An Introduction to Commodity Trust: Brands and Commodities

Without implying that the different dimensions of trust are perpetually in competition with each other (they are all vital to us and sometimes they *are* in competition), one of the dimensions – commodity trust – tends to dominate our lives more than any other. In fact, thanks to the impact of reification and devices, it dominates our lives almost entirely. From minute to minute, knowingly or unknowingly, willingly or unwillingly, at every turn, we allow commodity trust to restrict the choices we allow ourselves. As a result we force ourselves to make do with choosing from a restricted menu of options and ignore the wider degrees of freedom available to us. In close-up the commodity trust dimension of our model is as shown in Figure P4.1.

When we trust something other than a human being we are talking of some sort of commodity trust. We are trusting a product or an abstract proposition – very often, with our lives and with the lives of the people we love. Some choices might be trivial – say, the type of beer we choose in a supermarket. Some might be a little less trivial – say, the school we send our kids to. Others might be far from trivial – say, our long-term career choice. At some time or another, it's fair to say that entire futures – business, commercial, professional, social, economic, military, political – have clung on for dear life to a thread of commodity trust and survived. Some others have not been so lucky.

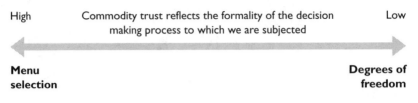

Figure P4.1

Commodity trust is the means by which the powerful network trust that cements together personal and relatively narrow groupings becomes extended to take in entire populations and global markets. In both a social and a business context, commodity trust is the essential cornerstone of stable cooperation, which is a little perplexing given, as we show in the next chapter, that commodity trust is itself intrinsically unstable.

What might be called the risk–reward nexus – the simple and well-known rule that high rewards only come with high risks – is clearly going to be part of any trust deal in which trust can always be taken advantage of and can always be abused. (Risks that are not 'worth the risk' are seldom taken.) Without question, this applies more powerfully to commodity trust than to any other of trust's dimensions. This is so if for no other reason than it entails a shift from a stance of cooperating through personal choice, over which some degree of personal control might be exercised, to a place where all practicalities of control are effectively given up and the assumption made that risk will be managed vicariously. Vicariousness is itself a huge risk in all its forms.

Its Power and Reach

Commodity trust is a powerful driver with lots of rewards and lots of risks for all the players involved. Most of history's wars, for example, share commodity trust as their common *casus belli*. Just as the Wars of the Roses pitted the commodity of York against that of Lancaster, and the Cold War communism against capitalism, so the crusades had previously done the same with competing religions and the Romans had fought for the commodity of order against barbarism.

Us versus them shooting wars at the time and place of writing are focused on the commodities we call civilization and terrorism.

Terrorism and shooting wars aside, today's basis for commodity trust is mainly presented to us in the form of brands. Brands exist to enroll consumers as foot soldiers in their campaigns for ascendancy in the war for exposure, control and market share. By our designer labels, our supermarket shopping choices, by the NASDAQ shares we buy, by where we eat our fast food, by the operating system on our laptops, by the budget airlines we use, by the cars we drive and the vacations we take, all of us are engaged at some level in struggles aimed at extending the effects of commodity trust.

Its Character

Commodity trust is rooted in people's basic disposition to cooperate with each other – we are social animals after all is said and done. As well as our sense of duty and our sense of self-preservation, moral, religious and ethical dimensions have been layered on to this disposition across countless generations (not to mention commercial, professional, economic and business requirements). As a result we have sets of expectations, and look for there to be some acceptable level of due process that satisfies them in places and institutions in which we invest our trust. Pointedly, when we do find them we often trust the process more than we trust the institution itself. (The medium after all, as we've already seen, is the message, a phenomenon that is at the heart of brands and branding.)

So to satisfy these expectations and to best exploit the risk–reward nexus in terms of brand associations, commodity trust is characterized by the formality of its decision-making processes. This characteristic alone enables us thoughtlessly to board a Boeing 747 or buy organic vegetables from a reputable source, or shop at an unfamiliar branch of a familiar chain store or invest in Big-Four-audited Blue Chip (formerly Big-Five-audited) stocks or send our credit card details to Amazon dot com.

By the same token, boarding a battered old airliner with no markings, no identifiable livery and no maker's name, buying GM vegetables from a street barrow, and shopping with, buying stock in and sending card details to the Here Today Gone Tomorrow Trading

Company dot com would severely test the extent of our commodity trust.

Its Price

Borgmann has shown us how commodification de-skills us at the same time as it extends our capabilities and makes our lives easier. And McLuhan has shown us that with the extension of capabilities comes amputation. The joint message, in other words, is nothing is for nothing and we all must pay a price for our role as infantrymen in our brands' armies. As we saw earlier, the price is what we give up. It is the forgone consumption economists call opportunity cost. For businesses that are heavily invested in commodity trust (that is, the majority of them) radical solutions are needed if these opportunities are to be profitably exploited. Radical solutions require simply an understanding of the difference between choice as menu selection and choice as degrees of freedom. We begin exploring these in the next chapter.

On an individual level the price we pay in trust terms is our acceptance that the choice the commodity offers us is wide enough to give us what we want. To be part of today's business world in any capacity – player, leader, entrepreneur, stakeholder, employee, consumer, even innocent bystander – entails giving up a set of choices that are outwith those offered by the brand as a result of its due diligence process. Thus are degrees of freedom curtailed and potential for trust abuse placed in the hands of some form of brand management that is vicariously exercised on our behalf. So, as a result, if your favourite store doesn't stock it, then you don't really need it and if your favourite airline doesn't fly there, then you don't really want to go there.

Such personal trivialities become brutally insignificant when commodity trust is extended to the global economy. Then the real war begins in earnest. J. K. Galbraith, in a 1991 London lecture entitled 'How we get the poor off our conscience', summed up the brutality when he said 'The thought that, in some undefined way, we must not hurt the economic system is still one of the most prominent means by which we get the poor off our conscience'.

In other words, the world is precisely the way it is not because of abusive systems but because of the misguided commodity trust we have collectively invested in those systems and the constrained choices we allow ourselves as a result.

Its Scope

Commodity trust, as the opening paragraph of this introduction makes clear, practically rules our lives. As a measure of its scope, that's useful in some respects and less useful in others. The significance is that it works not only in every context but also on every level. (And that's an important image to bear in mind. As the great Fred Herzberg said of his lucky horseshoe, 'it works whether I believe in it or not'.) So that everything that we write about commodity trust's applicability to a global concern applies equally to a sole trader (and even to the proverbial one-man band). Likewise, what applies to the Coldstream Guards applies to any guardsman taking one step forward.

The corner of Williams's four-box model from which we originally extrapolated our notion of commodity trust as one of trust's four dimensions is labeled *non-egoistic* and *macro*. *Non-egoistic*, as the label implies, means that generally it's really nothing personal in terms of choices we make, while *macro* means it occurs more often than not. That's a pretty close approximation to life itself, we reckon. As part of our verification process we looked at Zizek's work in a similar context. An overlay of his labels gave us *inconsistent* and *inauthentic*, an equally valid life view.

11

The Commodity Trust Deal
and its Effects

It is a sign of where we are with trust that often we find it easier to trust a thing than a person or an organization. We somehow assume that the absence of direct, and directly attributable, motivations in the thing concerned makes it impersonal and in some sense safer. For example, we have a tendency to prefer technical fixes to real solutions that involve change. Business will often pay far more for a 'proven' method than for an intelligent and experienced practitioner.

If we go back to our core definition of trust – that the object of trust will look after our interests – we seem to be saying that a passive thing is going to come closer to meeting our needs than a person will. This may be true in practice and in people's experience but it speaks to a devastating isolationism of our own making. And of course our assumptions about our future interests, needs and preferences rarely turn out to be accurate, so we leave ourselves with practically no possibility of an intelligent response to change.

The commodity trust deal between a supplier and a set of customers is basically one of 'if you don't ask any questions you won't be told any lies'. The nature of a commodity that is the subject of the trust deal is that it is not differentiated or fleshed out but is instead reduced to a set of parameters and a price. In doing so it gets reduced, without any real negotiation, to an easy option shortcut for the customer and an easy option line of business for the supplier.

The implication of this lack of negotiation and, going further back, education and interest in the product, is that, once made, the deal cannot be renegotiated. If there is something that the customer needs to know he or she is unlikely to be told, and both the customer and the supplier collude in this being the responsibility of the supplier, 'their business'. Access to crucial knowledge in this instance is likely to be among the forgone opportunities resulting from the choice. Quite simply, the deal is that the supplier does not bother the customer and this coincides with the supplier's business interests. It begs the question of the value of knowledge.

It is for this reason that we maintain that commodity trust is unstable. The customer will sooner or later feel let down or betrayed by the supplier and by the product. Sooner or later some need will arise such that the product cannot continue to meet the customer's real interests over time. When that happens and the deal cannot be renegotiated, it will fail. We think that the high level of customer disillusion and apathy towards marketing initiatives is probably due at root to this truth.

To be able to see the issues in commodity trust we need to establish a focal practice as described by Borgmann. Only from the perspective of something that is not already embedded in the set of commercial relationships can we see what commodity trust really brings in terms of reduced degrees of freedom and limited choices that matter. Commodity trust may still be viable and it will remain important in many areas of business but it needs to be removed from its taken-for-granted setting before it can be evaluated.

We have touched on food and food policy a number of times, and it is a useful metaphor here. Supposing our focal practice is growing and eating our own food. Everyone knows at some level that both the freshness and the involvement with soil and seasons bring a taste that simply cannot be bought. Through this perspective we have layer on layer of innovation and technical development in agricultural practices and food distribution that almost without exception take us away from the values inherent in the focal practice. The reduction of food to typical supermarket parameters of consistent size, shape and colour, availability through all seasons, long storage life, lack of blemishes etc., moves us away from the things we actually wanted. We get something that can be measured and managed that goes against our core concerns.

As a metaphor we can see that this is much more frequent than we might at first suppose. Instead of dealing with the strange and potentially unique values of customers, we build an abstract set of preferences that stand in for customer behaviour. It is this crucial step that leads to the instability of commodity trust.

Models and Systems

The World Bank needs poverty more than the poor need the World Bank, as FIFA needs football more than football clubs need FIFA. (Our guru note on J. M. Keynes, the great economist, provides a flavour of the thinking that led to this initial expression of Smith's Law.) In this piece of polemic, 'poverty' has been reified into a subject of academic study, something you can be a highly paid expert in, something that institutions can address with billion-dollar programmes with no sense of shame or irony. In such programmes there is zero risk that poverty will be eradicated and the experts find themselves out of a job. They are not alone.

> An anti-discrimination group has little motive to report improvement, or even stasis, in cultural relations, because that would lessen the perceived need for the group.
>
> Tim Cavanaugh, *Reason Magazine*,
> December 2002

In the world of social systems, we hardly notice when something has been reified. As a result virtually everything, including trust itself, *has been* reified.

A company's share price is a key piece of financial reification, allowing shares to be traded on stock markets without reference to the company or any of the underlying influences on that price. Investment in the company takes place via the rules of the market and in general only the prescribed public information such as accounts is available to investors. (Beyond, that is, that well-known and trusted commodity delivered by investment analysts.) Recent events have shown how far adrift the public face of a company can be from its underlying value. Even the concept of underlying value is a reification relative to the rich notions of value that might pertain to particular investors in particular circumstances.

Another way to look at this is to say that the notion of share price and trading in shares is a model of the underlying set of economic relationships. Life doesn't look like the model all the time: we have insider trading, we have corrupt accountants, we have PR of all sorts determined to put a suitable spin on the company's fortunes. The model is an idealization and the reification works to make it seem as though the model is the reality. The share price and its effects are real enough in terms of affecting power and actions. It is just that the model doesn't work in the ideal way in some circumstances. Cynically, we might say that the model works except when it doesn't, as the following illustration shows.

Money, Inflation, Certainty and Trust

Money is perhaps the world's pre-eminent commodity. In a business book that much should go without saying. Money, after all, as the song says, makes the world go round and it doesn't take an insight of a Galbraithian order to acknowledge that things are done in protection of money that are to the detriment of the majority of people.

Death and taxation are life's big two, if not its only two, certainties. That's according to the rich man's proverb of course. And, proverbial or otherwise, certainties, through the impact they have on risk, subtly alter the nature of trust. Crudely, where there's certainty, trusting is OK. Take away those certainties – make death and taxes optional, for example – and problems will definitely arise from changed trust. In the UK, up until quite recently, there was a third certainty that engaged us (it particularly engaged the rich). This was inflation. Changes to the big two are not available at the time of writing but factor inflation out of the equation and the problems start.

Inflation eats into the value of money and as a consequence it eats into the trust people have in money as a commodity. Apart from the basic price mechanism, the capitalist economic system has developed mechanisms aimed at countering the deteriorating value of money. Share markets are one such. In inflationary times holding money becomes like a game of pass the parcel. Players who can afford to do so aim to get out of it as rapidly as they can. Doing so by buying an appreciating asset with a depreciating commodity has proved over the recent past to be the 'free lunch' dream of mythology, a free lunch on which an entire financial services industry grew fat and prospered.

The dynamic was stunningly simple: thanks to inflation the value of inventories and work in progress rose for even the most inefficient operations and regardless of management inputs or business leadership. As they rose, share values rose and with them stock markets. Demand for shares drove up prices. Buyers' willingness to shed money further devalued it. The free lunch was so extensive that even ordinary people — those traditionally without excess disposable lumps of money — were able to pick up some scraps. The magic figure at the margin was the difference between the rate of inflation and the rate of interest. As long as returns on investment exceeded this difference any investment was considered good enough. Loans could be taken out to buy stocks secure in the knowledge that they would appreciate and that repayments would be made in a further devalued commodity. Generally, this cycle became the trusted measure of both efficiency and competitiveness.

Slaying dragons that have been ravaging the countryside for generations solves some problems but inevitably creates a whole set of new ones. Just as the end of the Cold War signaled the so-called end of history, so the decline of inflation exposed the true nature of markets' antics to counter inflation. Trust in counter-inflation mechanisms is clearly misplaced once the countryside-ravaging dragon of inflation has been slain. Further, when an examination of the nature of the mechanisms reveals them to be inefficient and misguided, it is only natural that questions come to be asked about other facets of the commodity trust we have placed in economic and financial systems. The confidence that is generally taken as the motive force of markets is a particular facet of this commodity trust. In the light of exposed inadequacies, it is small wonder that our confidence that the commodity will take good care of our financial futures and is therefore a good place to put our trust — and our money — is temporarily dented if not shattered forever.

Rebuilding Confidence

Markets are fortunate. Not only are we social animals who as a result tend to congregate in market places, we are also venal animals. So whenever there is money to be made, there will be a market. So markets, it may safely be predicted, will recover largely unreformed from practically any damage they suffer.

This means that the misguided perception that markets must somehow show themselves to be trustworthy in order to thrive is little different from them claiming to be safe havens in times of inflation. There are no safe havens – what trustworthiness there is, is discounted from the outset. There is only the risk–reward nexus.

There is only one authentic way for markets to make trust of any kind possible: a statement to the effect that a market's purpose is to enable those who are in possession of the best information to make money and to avoid losses. And in acknowledgement of that, market regulators are empowered to deliver severe punishment to those who illegally exploit the power that information gives them (providing, of course, that they can trap such behaviour).

That trustworthiness has little to do with commodity trust where markets are concerned will come as no surprise to anyone who has ever given trust a second thought. It should come as no surprise at all to anyone. One of the world's oldest and best-known proverbs attests to that: *caveat emptor*. Let the buyer beware.

When the chairman of Citibank was supporting research into complexity theory he is reported to have said that conventional economics gave him answers about all the unimportant times when equilibrium conditions held, and gave him no answers at all in the important times when equilibrium did not hold – the crises and the crashes. Our observation is that economics as a model has similar properties to the social systems and the operation of, for instance, commodity trust. We trust brands and corporations until we don't. All the work people do managing brands extends the time and the population for whom trust holds, and it necessarily amplifies the crash that occurs when people feel they have been manipulated and conned by the corporation concerned.

Marks & Spencer is the classic example of a retail company with exceptionally high trust from its customers and its suppliers. It had (has?) an exceptional reputation for the thoroughness and uncanny prescience of its planning system. The focus, however, on reified aspects of its performance allowed the whole enterprise to drift away from a viable customer offering without anyone paying attention. The result was a very public and painful crisis lasting several years, including a board succession crisis, a supplier crisis, a retrenchment from European markets, causing a major legal challenge, and an almost complete loss of image.

The public clamour is often for the reality to be made to look like the model. That this is Canute-like seems to escape most people's attention.

A Knowledge Management Case

A major defence contractor supplies, among other things, warships to the Navy. A class of warship has a design life of perhaps fifty years, going through several major and minor refits in that time. From a maintenance perspective there are six million distinct components to track: specifications, design rationale, interoperability, supply chain etc.

The Navy requires that this knowledge be managed to reduce the through life cost of the ships, and also requires that the knowledge be used as a partial basis for future projects. The defence contractor understands this as essentially a database issue: a model of the warship class can be developed that mirrors the reality and allows configuration issues to be understood.

That this model is inadequate is easily seen by looking at parallel programmes within the same contractor. They have essentially the same requirements from the Navy but no point of contact with other programmes: the way they view the same components and the design issues concerned is completely incompatible. So we can assume that over a fifty-year time span, political and management changes within the organization will result in the existing model being seen to be inadequate for all sorts of reasons. As above, and King Canute notwithstanding, the defence contractor is trying to homogenize practice across all its divisions so that these differences are ironed out.

The commodity trust that allows us to restrict our attention to a menu of choices and reifications instead of to the whole problem is inherently unstable because of the way models diverge from what they are intended to represent. Commodity trust is actually framed and underpinned by a power structure that allows a powerful player to constrain (possibly for mutual benefit) the choices of other players. We tend to lose sight of the fact that changes in the relationship make the menu invalid.

Reification and Rules

The main reason why models fail and reification lets us down is that people use the formal structure for their own ends in a way that can never be controlled. They are able to exploit the system precisely because of the way a model works, and it is the exploitation that causes the model to fail.

A classic case of this was Britain's involvement in the European Exchange Rate Mechanism (ERM). The ERM model was that by binding currencies together and supporting currencies within their trading bands, all the currencies in the system would be stabilized against exchange rate fluctuation. The very existence of the mechanism gave currency traders a chance to exploit the system. What they did was to pick the outsider that was least committed to the mechanism, the United Kingdom, and bet against the currency until it was forced out, thereby making huge speculative gains. There was no conspiracy, just a widespread understanding about how to play the system.

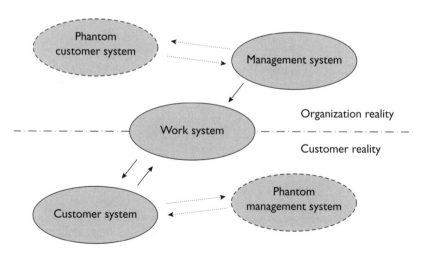

Figure 11.1 Customers and management do not see the same work system

Speculative gains in one part of the system are offset, of course, by the losses of those who had and maintained commodity trust in the ERM. The ERM as a political artefact of the EU was, of course, heavily entrenched in hierarchical trust, compelling people within the system to trust the ability of the political system to deliver the goods.

Within a business management system these effects are depicted tellingly in Figure 11.1. The customer needs that management sees are mediated via the organization's reality and result in a phantom customer system that cannot give real guidance as to what work needs to be done. There is a mirroring frustration in the phantom management system that does not allow customers to get their needs addressed.

12

Commodity Trust and Radical Brand Solutions

Sometimes it feels as though the whole world is reduced to commodities, supplied to generalized markets by generalized traders and with nominal price competition between producers. If something is a commodity its price is just about the most significant thing about it. Products and services that try to distinguish themselves on quality or image must avoid getting pulled into that commodity place. (It says much for the power, nature and ubiquity of commodity trust that practically its only known counter lies in establishing a unique selling proposition – the highly reified commodity we all know and love as USP.)

Part of the implication of commodification, with its attendant focus on price, is that trust in the product is already discounted. Very often we hear spokespeople from supermarkets lamenting the fact that people will only buy on price and that in the end you get what you pay for. This doesn't wash with the public, and it doesn't wash with the authors of this book.

The key point about commodities is that they recognize only the circumscribed choice determined and presented by the supplier. Sometimes you can only buy 'potatoes' for example, or 'cheddar', and sometime you can buy King Edwards, Charlotte or Picasso on the one hand or Davidstow, Baker's Extra Tasty or Tasmanian on the other. But there is always a finite list created by the supplier. And, if it should turn out that Baker's Extra Tasty was produced by child labour in Siberia rather than by thriving farmers in Somerset then trust has been breached no matter what price I as a consumer wanted to pay.

Indeed, the buying proposition of a commodity can be entirely spurious. We are used to the truism that nobody ever got fired for buying IBM. The brand came to stand for just that safety of business decision making. And the converse – that people *have* got fired for buying DEC or whoever else – is more illuminating. If you make a mistake (and the history of IT is littered with systems failures of all sorts) then, in many environments, you need to be able to defend your position and the decisions you took.

In gaining global dominance, IBM reportedly spent huge amounts of money manipulating the press and the judicial process in order to keep that basic sales proposition alive. It remained safe (for the purchasing manager) to buy IBM even if it was demonstrably a bad business choice that had already caused business damage elsewhere. This, of course, is not what the explicit brand and commodity proposition is or was.

Brands need to retain the trust of their consumers. This is almost a definition of a brand that is worth anything. The trouble comes about as a result of the brand owners having a huge economic incentive to maintain the brand even at the expense of the integrity of the proposition. The long and sorry history of the tobacco companies, one of many similar horror stories, drives this message home.

Commodities and Cash Cows

Conventional business wisdom shows us a product lifecycle, where development and marketing costs are incurred upfront for the sake of a period of sustained sales when the profits made readily repay the cost and reward the risk of the earlier parts of the cycle. This is commodification at work: the deliberate creation of some sort of standard product or service that can be made in large quantities and sold uncontroversially at a good rate of return.

This is explicitly the creation of a steady-state process, something that does not acknowledge change and risk. Brand owners and producers will make the point that the process does not work every time, that for every cow there are ten costly failures. Failures notwithstanding, in this process the commodity proposition is that there is no risk to the consumer because the supplier has already understood the risks and dealt with them. So, for example, you cannot buy certain types of unpasteurized cider in a supermarket because of the outside chance that a bottle will explode. Rather than share the risk with consumers for the sake of taste and choice, the option is removed from the list of commodities you are allowed to buy. In the limit the proposition is that the only risk a consumer can take is not to buy from this supplier.

As a trust proposition this is just about as asymmetric as it can get. The supplier does not trust the consumer about anything. In fact, the proposition works by explicit mistrust. Everything the consumer might do that might not be in the consumer's ultimate interest (as defined by the supplier) is either removed from the available list of choices or is the subject of explicit and often fatuous warnings:

These peanuts may contain nuts.

On the other hand, the consumer is expected to have blanket trust in the supplier about just about everything pertaining to the deal. My supermarket is less than a mile from a cherry orchard. The cherries in the supermarket are three times the price, stale and tasteless. There is less choice of variety and less assurance of production standards. But the brand proposition is that these supermarket cherries are the ones I should buy.

> The quandary commodity trust has presented throughout history, and which it continues to present, has almost become a commodity in itself. Countless authorities are available to justify whatever chosen stance is preferred. Mill's dictum, for example that 'no one has the right to interfere with me for my own good but only to prevent harm to others' appears on the face of it to be more than ample justification for every abuse of commodity trust there has ever been as well as for every clause in every piece of Health and Safety legislation. On the other hand, adherence to Wittgenstein's claim that 'no one can think a thought for me, just as no one can don my hat for me' seems bound to lead to altogether different outcomes.
>
> Guru guide: John Stuart Mill, English
> philosopher (1806–1873); Ludwig Wittenstein,
> Austrian philosopher (1889–1951)

Of course, the cash-cow proposition, whatever other benefits it might deliver, is not in the customer's best interest from the standpoint of price. Something is being sold for more than it needs to be if the customer's long-term interests were to be factored in. The pricing mechanism is not actually well suited to balancing the customer and supplier interests over the product lifecycle. The economic arguments push towards the establishment of a cash-cow product, which to maintain its status must avoid education of the customer in the wider issues of its production and use. The last thing an old-style IBM salesman ever wanted was someone who actually knew about computers and business systems.

Included in this need to avoid customer education are all aspects of risk and change. So we cannot have open debate about food safety issues because they call into question, and potentially threaten to undermine, the brand propositions of the products concerned. We certainly cannot have independent research into the side effects of technologies like GM (genetically modified) crops because the brand proposition has already discounted (or sidestepped) the possibility of there being a risk to the customer of the customer's behaviour in buying such products.

In terms of commodity trust, the dynamics accounting for impossibility of open debate on GM foods are the same dynamics that enable us to allow high-profile institutions of which we really have the right to expect better – police forces, palaces, crown institutions and so forth – to conduct their own 'internal inquiries' when failures in their processes actually get brought to light. 'Hold on to nurse for fear of worse' has long been passed down to us as good, if arguably constricting, advice. Commodity trust often proves to be a very cruel nurse.

The Supplier Perspective

The supplier perspective follows a similar, indeed mirroring, logic. If customers are going to blame the supplier for everything that can possibly go wrong, then clearly the range of customer propositions must be reduced to a manageable level. We cannot let the customers ask for just anything. The proposition must be framed in such a way that we – the suppliers – are the experts about the product and there are no obvious avenues of attack for knowledgeable customers.

We have to build consistency across the product range and the service proposition so that problems are seen to be isolated issues in a sea of competence, not straws in the wind indicating more widespread difficulties with still more to come. We will never shift the volume of goods we need to if we are challenged on a routine basis about what we are selling.

The difference between the customer and the supplier perspectives goes with the asymmetry of the trust: in the end the supplier has the initiative and must either extend trust to the customer or build a brand proposition that avoids *having* to trust the customer. The problem with brands and with commodities lies not in the concept but in the asymmetry of trust, which sets up a scenario guaranteed to end up with disappointment and mistrust much of the time. Radical brand strategies start by acknowledging this designed-in asymmetry. They quickly move on to doing something about it, making progress through an understanding of how degrees of freedom differ from menu options. Radical action starts when the trust deal changes to reflect this new knowledge.

The brand is not merely associated with cash-cow products but is a rod the customer can use, and does use, to beat up the supplier. (Ironically, when it comes to the buying and selling of brands, this asymmetric power imbalance gets neatly reified into 'goodwill' – the quaintly labelled anachronism that commodifies the brand's marketability and gives it its asset value.) It is the sense of having at least this much consumer power via the brand that the cynical customer uses to justify to himself his residual engagement with the brand proposition.

The Brand as Social Token

Commodity trust has enabled the cachet of a brand in recent years to be taken as a valid social identifier, as a way people can show their belonging to a certain group. (This is an extension of the network trust observation that began this section.) 'Cool Britannia' even used nation as brand in an attempt to raise the cachet of being British under New Labour.

Clearly there is a crossover into the territory of network trust where, rather than social opinions being a route to trust choices, brands are routes to social identification and to a certain sort of tribal exclusiveness. Our take on this is that brands are here trying to pre-empt the issue of network trust by coming before it and asserting their prior claims. A group of surfers with 'Fat Willy's Surf Shack' car stickers are unlikely, in this thinking, to be discussing how they were ripped off by Fat Willy. Their stickers are there partly to help them identify other surfers and partly to assert some part of their rebellious social identity. Their rebelliousness has already been colonized, almost before it is formed, by a brand asking to be trusted as the mediator of surfing needs.

When these issues extend to teenagers extorting money from parents, who can literally not afford it, for branded fashion items in order to be seen to belong to their social groupings we can see the abuse built in to this system. By subverting network trust between teenagers, which might in other times have built a critical perspective on the activities of these brand owners, the level of exploitation of the social systems that determine the fate of the supposed customers is raised to new heights. The brand passes from mistrust of the customer to outright disrespect and abuse. In any account their activities are not in the interest of their customers. Interestingly, this move was signalled by the move of the brand name from the inside to the outside garment label – the medium once again needing to be seen to be the message.

Blue Chip Blues

The business world has an elite often referred to as blue chip. The intended or accepted meaning is of a solidity, a membership of the business establishment that lowers the risk to people wanting to do business with them. So as an investor I get a steady return with no downside. And, given the chance, I am supposed to feel privileged to be a supplier. Blue chip is functioning here as a super-brand, something that guarantees the quality of the brands concerned.

The blue chip club behaves all in the same way – they have the same large companies as auditors, the same gang of marketing companies, the same ties into the political establishment. This is classic commodity trust behaviour: *trust us, we already take care of all relevant concerns.*

The days when companies had the economic, political and often monopolistic muscle to make the hubris stick are clearly gone. There is no company (arguably, in fact, no institution at all) now that cannot be swept away essentially overnight by the revelation that the measures it took to maintain appearances were not what they appeared to be. The claim to be blue chip is now a simple 'trust me' claim that any child has learned to question. We would now suspect that the larger a company is, the more chances there are to trip up and the less vigilant its managers are about abuses.

When it comes to super-brands in a commodity trust context, the 'rule of law' can be seen as the ultimate. Overarching everything we do, the notion that everyone is equal before it and no one is above it is, by any stretch of the imagination and in anybody's language, a pretty compelling trust deal. Although it is totally inauthentic in trust terms, as we will see a little later, it nevertheless addresses the asymmetry of its power thanks to the commodity we know as the common law. Through its case-based feedback, common law has, over the centuries, ensured that the rule of law today fairly closely reflects the consensual degrees of freedom of what we are pleased to call a civilized society. And will do so tomorrow too. Commodity trust will be a force for good while ever the rule of law prevails. I, for one, am glad. My feeling is that the common law is far too radical a solution to be implemented today if it didn't already exist.

Entrepreneurial Products

As we have noted earlier, it is often easier to see the trust propositions when we consider extreme entrepreneurial action. If we go back to the tradition of the inventor, who perseveres against all the odds with an idea whose time he thinks has come, we can see that there is trust flowing from the inventor to potential users of the invention. The inventor believes, rightly or wrongly, that when people finally engage with his idea, it will transform their lives. Users will be convinced and have cause to thank the inventor for his perseverance. This is trust. It is reasonably authentic trust because it flows from the inventor: he is not asking users to trust his brand proposition.

To get slightly closer to the mainstream, there are legends such as the Sony Walkman, where the original idea and product was launched against a background of market research that said that consumers had no interest and that there was no market. So products can create a market where they correctly interpret some tide in consumer interest, taste and activity patterns. The great breakthroughs are in some real sense history-making events. There was a time when consumers did not understand that they needed to be listening to music while moving around in public places.

So at the start of this cycle, the business looking for breakthrough has to trust its customers. There is no evidence of trustworthiness in the customers in the sense that they can be relied upon to evaluate and try out the breakthrough product, still less that they will buy it. Once the breakthrough has occurred, and the product is established as useful and desirable, then very quickly that initial step of customer trust is discounted, especially if this is a consumer situation.

We can now see that the lack of a relationship between customer and supplier that goes beyond commodity trust is also damaging to innovation. The breakthrough product has to have large market potential (even if there is no evidence) if a business is to take the risk of pursuing it. Without a relationship, that risk cannot be shared in any way with the customers for whose ultimate benefit the risk is to be taken. The ultimate risk belongs to the entrepreneur and an entrepreneur is someone who seeks out those risks for the sake of their significance. But the customer needs to be able to do more to stimulate this risk taking than merely to buy the product.

Businesses have moved to rather political modes of engagement like focus groups and statistical studies of customer behaviour, but to my eye these developments betray themselves as being commodity trust instruments. Nothing an individual says in such a context, no matter how insightful or how significant, has a way of being dealt with for what it is. It will either be buried in the inherent averaging and summarizing or it will be stolen and used without recourse to its author. None of these instruments seeks actual engagement, only arm's length data gathering.

The Market for Art

Perhaps nowhere are these conundrums clearer than in the market for the production and exchange of works of art. We hold simultaneously to the romantic image of the impoverished artist in his garret working as a slave to his genius and to the auctioning of established masterpieces at astronomical prices. The road from one image to the other, from someone completely out of contact with humanity and potential customers, to an auction whose dynamics rest on competitive acquisition, shows us how something can be simultaneously a commodity and the product of authentic trust. In these two universes, the artist searches for things of lasting significance to people he does not know and art lovers compete to own the products of that process, to be free to interpret that significance.

In this example the value to customers rests in the struggle of the producer, and the authenticity of that struggle is paramount. In ordinary commodity products we are asked to believe that the struggle is of no significance, that the value is entirely carried by the intrinsics of the product and by its image. To my mind this is always on the edge of being untrue, indeed impossible. Underlying the product has to be a sense that my interests are being taken care of by the producer and the merchant.

13

Commodity Trust in Contracts

The standard business response to the need for reliable relationships is the contract in all its many and varied forms. The contract itself is a commodity, and because it is so prevalent as a relationship mechanism, it is worth spending some time understanding its trust status and implications. By the same token, the whole area surrounding contracts offers rich pickings when it comes to radical strategies in business relationships. In particular, the contract contains sanctions and remedies for non-performance, which give people a feeling of comfort that their interests are at least underpinned in some way.

The basic need for a contract stems from a barter situation where the exchange in the barter is not instantaneous but separated over time. First I will do this for you and then, in return, you will do that for me. We both understand this as a fair exchange and we both want to complete the barter, but after I have provided you with my service or product there is a clear incentive for you to be opportunistic and omit to complete your part of the bargain. The contract provides evidence of the agreement and a sanction that I can apply to persuade you to complete the deal. As we move to typical commercial contracts, this evidence is often as simple as when payments are made for products and services: we have explicit but also merely implied contracts such as when you fill your car with fuel or harbour expectations regarding the fitness for purpose of a product.

This is clearly extremely important economically, and the effective working of a legal system to enforce commercial contracts in a way that is seen to be fair by the contracting parties is one of the determining factors in allowing economic growth. It is also undeniably a hallmark of civilized life. In corrupt or chaotic societies, where political disputes or economic mismanagement can disrupt commercial contracts arbitrarily, people do not take the commercial risks necessary to develop an economy. Without doubt this is an issue of trust.

To get a hint of an alternative view, however, we might look at societies where there is rampant recourse to litigation. Although this appears to be in the service of enforcing explicit and implicit contracts, it does not build economic activity and trust. It causes a similar waning of the willingness to be entrepreneurial and to take risks as its anarchic opposite. In our case illustration of the construction industry in the UK we have something of these features. It appears to be necessary to sue your suppliers before they sue you, whether or not there is an important underlying breach of contract.

We notice that contracts tend to be based on observable external outputs, and it is easy to see why. This is a commodity trust application, where the parties collude to believe that it is the product and service that count in the exchange, and that so long as these things meet the agreed specification there isn't a problem. Even when the specification and related contract elaborate themselves into filing cabinets full of unreadable text, people don't seem to twig to the possibility that they are barking up the wrong tree.

The Case of the Fantasy Medical System

To see how strong this illusion can be, consider this story told by an arbitrator in the USA about an IT services company supplying a system for sharing best practice surgical procedures among a group of hospitals.

The client, the group of hospitals, was going to arbitration because – having spent around a million dollars on development – they had found that the system did not work. My colleague was expecting to look at the specification for the system to assess how much of what had been asked for had been delivered and what still needed to be done.

Over a period of weeks there were delays and excuses in sending documentation to support the arbitration, and finally the client withdrew. There was no specification, no material description of what was to be built or how it might be assessed. And yet the client was happy to invoke a legal procedure to defend his rights as though legal intuition could determine arbitrary non-performance.

The confusion here is between relationship and commercial relationship. The commercial relationship, as abstracted – reified – into a contract, is just that – a set of commercial terms and arrangements. As a shortcut, in the great majority of our dealings as business actors or as consumers we allow the commercial relationship to stand in for the actual relationship. There is a confluence here of commodity and authority trust. We have commodity trust in what we procure and we have authority trust in the legal system to protect our interests where the commodity trust breaks down. When the legal system fails us there are generally howls of protest and the start of a political process to repair the damage.

It is not only in commercial law and contract where this is felt. Proponents of capital punishment for many years argued that it was better to dispatch the guilty rapidly rather than risk having to release and compensate them after their release from incarceration should subsequent evidence reveal them to be innocent and the processes of the law flawed. Despite being arguably as extreme as abuse of commodity trust can get, the argument has in fact been trotted out as recently as the release of the (highly reified) 'Birmingham Six' (freed in 1991 after eleven years of wrongful imprisonment).

The Other Way Up

It is perfectly possible to do things the other way up. Most of the business contracts I have signed have been on the basis that if the contract ever needed to be invoked then the relationship would already have failed: the contract is there to make clearing up after breakdown a little less messy. It is understood that there is a higher-level, relationship-based agreement that all parties will go the extra mile, and that when things don't work out as planned both ongoing commitments and payment schedules are simply walked away from. One colleague explicitly briefs his clients that they need not pay for anything that was not good value with hindsight.

The nub of the issue is whether sanctions are worth having. My own small company in its relationships with economically powerful clients has no practical use for sanctions. In effect the law does not provide me with a service. Conversely, I have to be circumspect about the same clients looking to raise some windfall money from my professional indemnity insurance policy. I have been asked more than once at contracting time how much I could be sued for.

If we go back to our original and basic point about deferred exchange, most of the time we end up relying on, if not trusting, our commercial partners. Quite often, big companies get a bad reputation for not paying their bills promptly, and many small suppliers refuse to supply on that basis. So, as far as this book is concerned, it is more fruitful to look at the nature of the necessary trust relationships and to enhance the ability of the trust to carry the needs of the parties. This is unlikely to be universally successful, but at least it deals with the nub of the issues rather than erecting a superstructure of other relationships.

There is a strong cultural aversion to taking this route. People who build an ability to collaborate and generate action are often punished when their work comes unstuck in some way. The culture wants legal safeguards even if in business terms these are not effective. The positive interpretation of this is that it is only from a position of visible strength that negotiation towards trust can take place. The negative interpretation is that people put their political and social safety ahead of the work every time.

All this exposes the ragged edges of the commercial framework that the law is supposed to underpin. So let's turn next to the authority trust in the law that is available to us.

The Legal Side of Contracts

The law does not work as a commodity trust mechanism: if it costs me more to use the law than I can recover using its services, that is no concern to the law. The law's view of itself is as the guardian of the meaning and interpretation of a set of rules and cases. Its version of justice is internally defined, not socially defined. If I trust the law, I trust it on its own terms and not on mine. It has zero authenticity because it cannot respond to the particulars of a situation outside the existing interpretation of such cases.

Of course, the use of legal mechanisms is not independent of relationship development. To the extent that I use legal threats I am clearly not building trust and collaboration. Several times in my career, close collaborators have, under pressure, taken a legal stance. The effect of this is to close the route of negotiation because both information and position become legal ammunition, whether that is the intention of the parties or not. The law forces you to fight and defend, whether that was your inclination or not. In a world of authority trust there is only right and wrong, victor and vanquished.

Hedging these issues is very difficult. We see Invitations to Negotiate issued by organizations wanting to partner to deliver services. The partnering words talk about joint delivery, joint objectives and sharing commercial risk. The questionnaire to evaluate potential partners talks about which risks will be borne by which partner, in a clear invitation to take unilateral commercial risk. We are so deeply embedded in a culture that sees value emerging from competitive pressure on price, that our legal framework really doesn't recognize other sources of value.

The experiments that have been conducted in the construction industry into other forms of association between companies – associations that allow the real construction risks to be managed ahead of the commercial risks between partners – are incurring huge overheads in constructing legal frameworks that do not interfere with what they are trying to do. And still we have the spectacle of people from the same set of companies being partners and promoting each other's interests in one context and in a parallel context indulging in the usual cut and thrust of legal opportunism. How can this be?

Combining the Worlds

It should be clear that these worlds of authentic trust, commodity trust and authority trust are deeply inconsistent but must coexist. We cannot tidy up this picture and make everything fit. These are different and mutually exclusive views of reality. They are deeply culturally embedded and take little account of each other.

Imagine you are an entrepreneur starting a project with huge commercial potential. You need the project to be successful and to access that potential. You need to use legal mechanisms to protect the intellectual property rights (IPR) that result. And you need your product to be trusted by its users. If you do not get the issues sorted, the advice given by your lawyer about IPR will ruin the authentic trust between the project members. The marketing of the product in different cultures around the world will raise commodity trust issues that will also split the team if they are allowed to. What you need is a lawyer who knows when to keep the law out of the way, marketing people who know that their insights are local, not general, and project members who know that their personal interaction has to deal with external realities that are literally foreign to them, to name but a few. This is all part of dealing with the world as it is while retaining the important degrees of freedom. Without freedom to act you do not have a project: it is impossible to be entrepreneurial without reinterpreting the rules as well as working with them.

Almost by definition, you cannot build effective relationships within these contradictions without dealing with the contradictions. The assumptions that the different worlds make about those relationships are never irrelevant, and constitute risk to the relationship if they are not factored in to the work. What people assume you are doing will never map to what you are doing without some work, especially if you are trying to change things. Sometimes it is important to work with the grain; sometimes it is important to refuse to. The distinction comes in the frame of reference you are using, and we suggest that relationships and trust within them form a suitably radical frame.

PART 5

Managing the Different Sorts of Trust

In the concluding chapters, we describe how abstractions about the way trust works get brought into the real world as pieces of work delivering business improvement. To make progress in understanding trust and a trust-based approach to managing risk, we need briefly to consolidate our understanding of the sorts of trust we need to promote and influence. Figure P5.1 represents the space in which this work must take place.

Bounded by the four sorts of trust – no one of which can ever exist in isolation – its contention is that business improvement is always available to the right and upwards of the current position.

A Gestalt View of Different Types of Trust

I was struck by two garment labels giving washing instructions:

- Wash dark colours separately
- Wash dark colours together

Despite being apparent opposites, they actually imply precisely the same action. And despite nominally being pieces of consumer guidance, without knowing about the hazards of washing machines they are probably both completely useless:

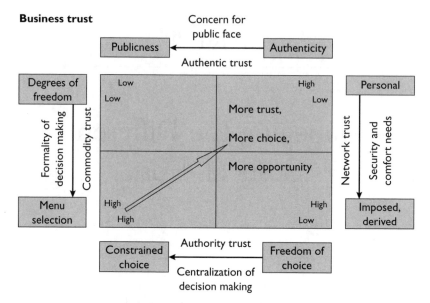

Figure P5.1   The different sorts of trust

Separate from what and together with what?

We have characterized four different sorts of trust, and we separate them because they have different properties that we need to understand: some are light and some are dark. While separate and labelled things may appear to be different, we need to keep in mind that they are all trust and all rooted in the same individual and group behaviour. We are going to wash them separately and together. When we emphasize a particular sort of trust, we are adding emphasis and not insisting on a hard and fast separation. Trust is about stable cooperation, and cooperation is stable for whatever combination of reasons it is.

The Types of Trust

Authentic trust is a personal thing. It is the trust we give to others because that is how we are and that is the choice that we make. It comes from our own sense of self and relationship and is not

MANAGING DIFFERENT SORTS OF TRUST 195

instrumental, not 'for' anything. Authentic trust is the only aspect of trust that is not (and cannot be) in some way imposed on us from outside. Personal as it is, authentic trust nevertheless always implies trusting *someone* or *something*. In doing so we give up a measure of power over ourselves and become open to the influences and leverage that exist in trust's other dimensions.

Network trust is the trust we place in those around us, our herd thinking and protection. When we don't know what to think, we reflect on others' insights and experience to clue ourselves into a trust position.

Authority trust is the principled and historical trust we place in the institutions and those in power to exercise that power fairly and not to abuse our lack of sanction. When we are told 'that's just the way things are around here' we have to decide how we will deal with the trust implications of that.

Commodity trust is the trust we place in a proposition or a brand, some abstract service and the things that underpin it. When we are thrown into a situation, perhaps mugged in the street, we trust the policeman to deal with the situation, or we don't.

Dimensions alone, though, are not enough. As we saw in detail earlier, trust works through reification. Each of its dimensions gives us something (extends) and in return takes something away (amputates). We reify things – situations, organizations, institutions, teams, people, brand, emblems – to give them a concreteness we find easier to relate to or categorize than their actuality. In doing so our reifications extend us – generally they make life easier for us or raise the platform from which we view the world. The price we pay for this is to lose – have amputated – something of our capacity for seeing things as they actually are.

In this context trust is itself a reification. So are its dimensions set out above:

(1) Authentic trust extends us to be ourselves while amputating the necessity of maintaining a public face that is likely at some remove to be phoney.
(2) Network trust extends us with a sense of belonging while subjugating our personal values to those of the group.
(3) Authority trust amputates much of our freedom of choice when we take our place in a hierarchy. It extends the power we have over those below us.

(4) Commodity trust extends our access to economies of scale. In return for the resulting menu options presented to us we forego degrees of freedom.

Trust in Action

As a preliminary step from the abstract to the real worlds we can look at a situation and decide which trust dimensions to explore first as a beginning to analysing the situation further. Since we are always asking what it is that stabilizes a situation and the cooperation between the people in that situation, the influences of reification, amputation and extension can never be ignored. Table P5.1 gives a flavour of this. We can look at the barriers to different sorts of trust – for instance of trying to develop authentic trust in the legal context illustrated.

The Gestalt of the Context

Flemons tells the story of a western student of Zen training in a monastery in Japan. The discipline of the monastery involved very manual gardening and much meditation practice. After a while the student, with trepidation and respect, approached the head of the monastery to point out some improvements in gardening practice which would save a great deal of time. The reply was that the student had not even begun to understand. If gardening took less time, there would be more time for meditation, and these things were in balance as they were.

The purpose of a system is what it does, and the trust that keeps the system working is relative to that purpose. So the context for trust is the setting within which the relevant relationships sit.

> We cannot work on trust without working on the system and we cannot work on the system without working on trust.

As with the student of Zen, that does not mean that many people think it a good idea to deal with these issues separately.

Table P5.1 Trust in action

Situation	Reification and extension	Foreground trust	Background trust	Choice implications
Consumer: the supermarket shopper	High reification, restriction to menu choice	Commodity trust in brands	Network trust in other consumers	Give up authentic values
Legal dispute	Low reification, imposed reality	Authority trust in law	Commodity trust in the rule of law	Submit to judgement
Buying technology	High extension and amputation	Network trust in user community	Authority trust in science	Give up control over process
Composing music	Low reification	Authentic trust in audience	Commodity trust in publisher	Allow interpretation of other musicians
Joining business organization	Reification of business, low extension	Authority trust in business	Authentic trust in new colleagues	Accept imposed model of behaviour

14

The Philosophy of Managing Risk

In common business parlance a risk, with hindsight, is simply the thing that prevented you from reaching your goal. The subtext is that if you had known in advance about it and had managed your affairs appropriately, you would have reached your goal.

So we get an implicit definition of risk management, which is:

> to manage the things that otherwise you might have left out.

If you think that doesn't make a lot of sense, then read on.

In doing work of any sort in any organization, there is an official, or maybe consensus, way to approach it. This approach includes certain things and by doing so excludes certain others. On many occasions the exclusion is appropriate and useful to getting the work done, and on many occasions it is inappropriate and amounts to a repression of a part of the work or its context. The received wisdom is that things that are repressed come back to bite. So we presume, and have observed in practice, a wide range of 'risks' that are intrinsic to the problem but have been repressed in the attempted solution. At its most trivial, we could quote 'more haste, less speed'.

Now the philosophical implications of this state of affairs are subtle. The power structure that provides or imposes the preferred approach is usually the same power structure that wants the problem solved or the work done. That is, there is usually no separation between the desired outcome and the route to that outcome. Despite much rhetoric to the contrary, the outcome and the route are not separate. So what would it mean to ask for risk management to be performed? The request seems to be paradoxical:

'Please take care of the parts of the problem I have excluded from the requested solution.'

It is for this reason that risk management tends to be strongly externalized – risks are things out there waiting to surprise us, they have nothing to do with us but we need to know about them so as to control them.

To see this from a positive rather than a negative perspective, consider the injunction below:

'You must take a risk before you can manage it.'

If you identify an uncertainty, a place where accidents might happen, something you depend on but cannot control, then you can deliberately engage with it as a risk to your outcomes. You would do so, of course, precisely because you want success with the outcomes.

Management and Risk Management

To manage a project or initiative is to work towards the goal, to do everything that is necessary to get there. To manage risk is to explore what is not being paid attention to, what has not been taken into account, ways in which the best laid plans of mice and men gang aft agley. Working outwards, we can see that these are not opposites but strictly complementary: one is the positive 'we must achieve this' and one is the negative 'we must not achieve this'.

So some things get expressed, some repressed. In talking of repression we could see that managerial definition of what was to be achieved could easily supply part of the risk as well as part of the solution. Equally, an understanding of context and of the way the world works, studied to enable risk management, may supply part of the essential solution as well as enabling management of risks *per se*. To get to the outcomes it seems necessary to pay attention both to what we think we must do and to what we think we can neglect or avoid. Both positive and negative contain vital information: if we foreground management, then risk management is the necessary background. If we foreground risk management, then the background must be management. If we can nimbly change our perspective at will, then we will be dealing with whole problems, not managerial abstractions and distinctions.

Trust as a Precondition

If I say I must get to place A and want your support, it takes a special kind of relationship if you are to go off and study place B. If I am to do risk management for you, or you for me, then we truly have to celebrate our difference. We have to understand that A is not B, and that A and B are inextricably related and joined. The ability to take opposing views, to think in opposite ways, to spend time on radically different priorities, we could call trust. Only by extending trust to you can I engage the part of your abilities that is opposite to mine, and only by engaging with difference can we do risk management.

In doing a project or an initiative we are dividing the situation, the context into some privileged priority concerns and some relegated concerns. Risk management says that, paradoxically, someone must spend time with the relegated concerns in order for the priority concerns to be effectively dealt with.

Nothing is really separate, we just choose to regard it as separate, and therefore we must deal with the effects of this rift in the wholeness of the context. It is the immediacy of the priority concerns that calls for trust. If I am being mugged in the street, my priority is to deal with the mugger, and the mugger's context can wait. Without the trust for someone to look at that context for long-term solutions to mugging then a spiral of violence may result.

In an organizational management context, to say to a senior manager who wants something done that it is really important to look at the effects of not doing it takes trust on both sides. Power wants to impose its view on the world and to set priorities absolutely and unilaterally. It wants at best to proceed with a consensus and a 'bought into' solution. Organizational trust is needed to keep minority opinions alive and to encourage diverse interpretations of the meaning of what is going on.

Decisions about Trust

Suppose I take some important action, or that something significant happens to me. Notice that language already forces me to distinguish between the active and the passive case. When I consider the significance of what has happened I tell three stories about it:

(1) I tell an external story that interprets the event in a way that protects any internal doubts or vulnerabilities I may have. This story often locates difficult aspects of the event in other people.
(2) I tell an internal story that justifies things to me. This story may concern itself with shame and guilt or with preserving an image of a frustrated better self.
(3) I tell, or maybe don't tell, a third or core story that contains the reasons why the other two stories get told. This third story is authentic with respect to the other two, which concentrate on packaging and presentation at the expense of staying in touch with the original event.

We can repeat this analysis at the level of group and organization. If anything, the effects become stronger with a larger body of people. The self of a group is often more primitive in its working and its ability to reflect on itself than the individual person.

This effect maps on to the scale of human 'being'. The more public we are in our actions and their justifications, the less easy they are to reference to that authentic experience of events. The internal story shows that to an extent we are our own 'public' and that the ability to reference authentic experience is something that needs to be developed, or recovered, or made space for.

The dimension of authentic trust in our model shows how authentic trust parallels the ability to reference authentic experience. This sounds like a truism but is actually quite profound. Unless I can pay attention to what something means to me, and what it means to me at some authentic level, not to some persona I need to project and hide behind, then I cannot extend trust authentically to another person. If the trust I extend belongs to a persona that is itself the creature of my need for security and comfort then it is actually of little use to its recipient.

We could frame an authentic trust proposition:

> Authentic trust can only exist to the extent that external forces and public pressure do not act to separate me from my authentic experience of events.

To some extent this is a question of internal stature. The ability of great figures to reference their own authenticity despite intense pressure is clearly one key to their ability to shape events around them.

Suppose now that I am part of multiple networks of colleagues, friends and acquaintances, social institutions and whatever. When things are going well for me I can play an active role in these networks, or not, as I choose. I can explore issues with friends or I can be private. When I am under pressure of some sort, these choices are not as available. I may need support and reassurance from those around me.

The choices that are in front of me when I am under pressure are about belonging:

(1) I may feel that solidarity with a certain group or their opinions improves my ability to withstand the pressure I am under. The pressure might be financial, but it might equally be pressure to think in a certain way, to support or oppose some faction in a developing political situation.
(2) I may feel an outsider in the way I perceive my reaction to events compared with that of those around me. But precisely because of the isolation of this position I may need to concur with majority opinion and to go along with majority judgements about the significance of events.

In any event, the question of security and comfort in my relationship with myself and the world raises questions about the behaviour of groups and networks that I am a part of. What do *they* trust and rely on? What are *they* assuming will be the fallout from these events? I have only finite ability to hold to a position different from that of those around me.

Since these relationships between myself and others are actually reciprocal, I have to extend my analysis to consider the security and comfort needs of others. There is always a theoretical possibility that we, jointly, are acting as a nervous herd, reacting to the slightest disturbance and never really understanding the source of the threat. My own need for comfort and security will raise that of others around me and theirs in turn will raise my own. To what degree do I trust my own judgement and to what degree do I rely on the herd?

Our network trust proposition might be:

> Network trust allows us to share the judgement calls of those around us, and needs for security and comfort drive us to rely on their support.

Where social relationships have been undermined or destroyed, network trust may not be available at all. It is possible for power relations to make it impossible to trust others, as their position becomes as distorted and fearful as our own. Societies vary considerably in their ability to develop network trust.

Suppose now that the issue is the degree to which I am able to choose a path. There are plenty of institutions – of which the law is the exemplar – that do not admit the individuality and particularity of context but insist on a single truth. Some of these are overt and explicit about the choices that they constrain or prohibit, and some are much more insidious in their mode of operation.

The issue of trust is now the degree to which I trust the institutions that have this behaviour. If I trust the law to be fair and liberal I may welcome the general restriction of choice that flows from its operation. If I do not trust the law I find myself with very few avenues to address issues that may be of crucial importance to me. The nature of the law and similar institutions is to deny any avenue to people who choose not to use the route provided.

Submitting to the hierarchical power of the institution and yet maintaining a grounded perspective on the effects of that submission are almost impossible to hold together. The institution will decide issues against its own principles, or lack of them, without regard to their impact on individual cases. The centralization of decision making in institutions implies that for good or ill the context will be averaged and generalized. People who inhabit this sort of environment for a long time lose touch with the possibility that there are other ways to see the world than the way the institution does.

In the extreme, my choice is limited to:

(1) Dealing only with the set of choices that are deemed legitimate by the particular hierarchy or hierarchies that claim my allegiance. I am no more and no less than I am allowed to be: 'he who is not for us is against us'.
(2) Resisting the demands of these hierarchies and being punished for doing so, no matter what that punishment amounts to. We may be talking about a hegemony of ideas that labels you mad if you think otherwise, we may be talking about treason, or we may be talking about being unable to buy a particular food because the supermarkets have taken up all productive capacity in another direction.

The authority trust question is simply 'yes' or 'no', always heavily loaded to get a 'yes'. Because people understand this dynamic, when governments say 'trust me' they generally produce the reverse of the effect they expect and demand. Authority trust is never about the evidence, it is about the demand. Until someone gets his tank off your lawn, there is no sense in questions about evidence and trustworthiness.

Our authority trust proposition might be:

> Authority trust commands us to surrender our individual concerns and judgement to the organizing power of a central authority, for our own good as defined by that authority.

Where power has been abused, this command can put people in a terrible situation that can easily destroy them. When the Mafia want to extend their protection to your business you have an unenviable choice – an offer you can't refuse.

Finally, suppose that I am faced with a consumerist world where there is on the face of it a huge array of choice in the products and services I can buy. In many parts of the world I can rely to considerable degree on claims made about these products and services. Sometimes it feels, however, as though the range of choice conceals common exclusions of choice; sometimes the more clothes shops I visit, the more I can become convinced that nobody is offering what I want to buy.

The trust issue now is whether in generating this array of choice the producers have taken my key interests to heart. If I choose an investment company to handle my personal pension, will the management of that company respect my choice and the reasons for it when selling out to another larger company? I contribute to their success. Is that a one-way street or do they owe me something in return?

My choices are now:

(1) Do I content myself with making selections from the array of commodity choices before me, trusting in the supply chain and the market mechanisms in place to deliver something that meets my needs? Will the fact that I and others like me have a need for certain things to be taken care of automatically deliver the provision of the appropriate product or service?

(2) Do I need to go behind the façade of 'the customer is always right' to check that assumptions I might make are actually borne out? Do I need to worry about what happens when the scenario changes and the suppliers I have committed myself to find themselves pushed into other choices? Can I rely on the regulatory frameworks to protect my interests?

Sometimes decision making is highly formalized and explicit. In these situations selection from the offerings available is the only game. If contractors tender for a piece of work the expectation is that one of them will get the work on the basis of the tender put forward.

Sometimes it is more important to exercise real choice that is intended to have long-term consequences for the outcomes in a situation. I might meet a service provider who is so open and imaginative that I positively make space to use them, sure that the partnership will provide opportunities for both parties. I could not justify this type of decision against a formal framework but many times it will be more effective than a more formal choice.

The commodity trust proposition might be:

Commodity trust allows the price of supply to fall, the convenience of supply to increase so long as there is a collective absence of interest in the means of production.

Commodity trust can take a dive, as during a food scare, and it can be damaged longer term as with the use of call centres. We inevitably learn from events and from experience whether certain practices are in our consumer interest. A generalized sense of nervousness about the bargain we have struck as consumers leads to an exaggerated suspicion once there are revelations that trust may have been abused.

The Quick and the Dead,
aka the Extended and the Amputated:
a Question of Opportunity Risk

There is a game theory concept of the stag hunt. If you want to catch and kill a stag to get fed, you need to collaborate with others and then you need to share the meat. Since you cannot catch the stag on your own this defines some rules, and if you need to collaborate with the same people again to catch your next stag, the rules about fair play proliferate.

Q: Why do we create systems of rules?
A: Because life is a stag hunt (see below for the longer alternative answer).

Q: What is the real power of processes that we create and then must fit into?
A: More people get to eat than would eat otherwise.

Q: What is the risk of this sort of behaviour?
A: Unintended or non-negotiable amputation.

Q: What is the risk of not systematizing our lives in this way?
A: Forgone extension.

At one level we create systems of rules and join organizations both to achieve something and to avoid something. We form a pact in which we give up some of our autonomy to regain some power, including economic power but also a sense of group agency (inconsistent, non-egoistic trust in our model). What we never understand in forming that pact is just what we are buying into, what the effect on us of the organization will be. So we are blindly following the steps set out by Maslow and we are bound to do this because 'only motivators motivate'. This is probably as close as I can get to an authentic answer to the first rhetorical question.

To do work we must take risks – real work does not have an assured outcome. One of the core values of business is risk taking (the problem is just that very often the managers who think of themselves as taking risks often do so at the un-negotiated expense of others). Amputated power to negotiate – to whistle-blow, even to complain – is part of the organization's entry ticket. This is why organizations do not like trade unions. And it is why there is no trust between them. So when we join with others in an organization to do work, to gain that sense of agency, we implicitly take joint risks (we have opportunity risks taken on our behalf) that never fall equally across the members of the organization. The meaning of power in organizations is largely one of who gets to take the hit.

The nature of systems of rules and of formal processes is that they make some factors in this pact that we make explicit and they hide others. (This is where reification comes in, followed by commodity trust aimed at closing out alternatives.) Typically they make our duties plain and they hide modes of power and of failure. You are not supposed to ask what happens when the system produces bad outcomes; at least you are only allowed to do so if you 'own' a process. Many formal systems have no effective ownership anyway. (Authority trust and the power of the hierarchy are the unquestionable surrogates.)

The rules and systems were set up precisely to structure the game, to make, in the view of its creators, certain favoured outcomes more likely and certain problematical outcomes less likely. But the creators of the game were neither all-seeing nor all-beneficent. Games are always political acts (and political acts are always games) that favour certain groups against others. So when someone questions whether the game buys its creators what they thought they were buying, it is a doubly political act: it challenges both the political legitimacy and the competence of the creators of the system. It also sets the beneficiaries of the system against the losers in looking at the game (amputation through opportunity risk is revealed) that was supposed to merely simplify their lives. If you are unlucky several groups think they gain by the game because they understand how to play it to their partisan advantage.

A Second Iteration

When we join an organization to do some work, we engage with various existing systems that structure the game that we must play. In the nature of things this both restricts and extends what we must pay attention to. The world (which is in actuality densely connected) has been partitioned for us so that we can add our exertions in a particular place and particular fashion, but the nature of the partitioning affects the risks we must take (and, as a result, the possible outcomes). It is never the case that we have an explicit agreement with the creators of the rules and the system about the effect of the partitioning. We are forced in effect to take an act of faith in order to work within the system and to try to understand its workings (opportunity risk implies TINA – There Is No Alternative).

As ever, the nature of this act of faith and the risk it entails is not acknowledged. It is problematical to turn it into a positive act, an act of trust, because the source of the risk does not acknowledge itself as such, if indeed there is any process ownership to be found.

At this point we can see a definition of living and dead systems vital to the work we do in the concluding chapters:

(1) A living system acknowledges that it is contingent on the actions and beliefs of the people within it, and so can be related to in a human way.
(2) A dead system is taken by people within it to be independent of their actions and beliefs and therefore cannot be related to in a human way.

15

The Cultural Foundations of Trust

We have stressed that trust is about very significant business decisions. The style of those decisions is often a cultural issue. In some cultures it is OK to find ways of making progress and in others it is more important to be seen to be tough or cynical or hypocritically cordial. So whether it is OK to try to find a route via trust is already an issue and may be a determining factor. We have stressed that there are always better outcomes available, but the route to those outcomes may be culturally unacceptable in many cases.

The reason why the route to trust may be culturally unacceptable is partly historical accident and partly to do with the issues it may raise. As we have said, trust brings multiple perspectives, belonging to the multiple stakeholders involved, to bear on the situation. The perspectives that other people bring – their views of us and our actions – are often uncomfortable: how could it be otherwise? It is part of trust to deal with these things. So cultures that repel such perspectives by their aggression or cynicism are going to resist routes to trust.

Similarly, unitary cultures that believe in the one correct view of reality are going to have difficulty dealing with the reality of alternative perspectives. Companies that have been in monopoly situations often tend towards this culture.

A Historical Conundrum for the Banks

The development of the banking system has included the development of card technologies for use as credit and debit cards. The banks
have developed the technologies and dealt with the issues of security
and fraud as they came up. Some of their solution has been around
technologies and processes and some has been around the way the
organizational power is deployed. To illustrate the former, consider
the history of automated teller machines (ATMs) for dispensing cash.
The banks were so sure when they were first deployed that these
systems were completely secure that any problems were deemed to
be automatically the customer's fault. Until of course it was demonstrated that attacks were possible and were being successful, when
extra security measures had to be introduced. To illustrate the second,
consider the VISA organization, which administers the VISA card
system and is run exclusively by and for banks. Any conditions
or charges levied by the organization are essentially impossible for
merchants or customers to resist.

There are now many consortia around the world developing multi-
application smartcard schemes. These allow smartcards to be used for
many purposes – to access transport, to authenticate access to government services, to register at college etc. Where there is 'stored value'
– that is, cash – on the card that can be debited by applications,
there are strong legal safeguards in most countries. In the UK these
are called capital adequacy regulations and relate to the liquidity of
the organization underwriting the cash on the cards. The natural
partners for such schemes to meet these regulations are the banks.

> Faced with the choice between changing one's mind and
> proving there's no need to do so, almost everybody gets busy
> on the proof.
>
> J. K. Galbraith

> A long habit of not thinking a thing wrong gives it a super-
> ficial appearance of being right and raises, at first, a formidable
> outcry in defence of custom.
>
> *Common Sense*, Tom Paine, 1776

However, the banks' experience tells them that to make the scheme
secure they have to own it. They, in their own estimation, are the

only people who understand practical security issues and they are not going to put their money at risk in becoming a partner to a scheme without it being their own scheme. This, of course, is a dead end and in practice banks in the UK have flunked negotiations. However, schemes are going ahead and will find a way around the regulations, by acquiring banking licenses if necessary. They will then challenge the banks in terms of how they construe customer need in making cash more useful and less hassle at the point of use (for many stake-holders, not just consumers).

There is a rider to this tale. The government in the UK is keen that all citizens should have a bank account, for various reasons to do with automated payment of benefits and fraud reduction. The banks have assessed that the cost of providing bank accounts to people on low incomes and on benefits is too high: they cannot see how to make money. But a major driver for smartcard schemes is the provision of universal access to e-government services and targeted subsidies to, for instance, transport. There has to be a business case for squaring this circle, but the cultural approach of the banks and the government makes it unavailable. This is a classic trust issue. There are considerable business rewards to the company that can take the leadership position.

The Political Moment

There is no trust from a utilitarian perspective. Trust and utilitarian values are contradictory and mutually exclusive. A utilitarian culture does not and cannot put relationships first. As we have shown many times, trust enables better outcomes than utilitarian perspectives, but that remains a deep paradox. Why cannot utilitarian values deliver utilitarian ends?

Utilitarian cultures, ways of arguing about what to do next and how to prioritize, have spread from the corporate world to most aspects of public, and even private, life. In doing so they have both exposed corporate life as absurd but also drained the available resources for doing anything differently. How would you make a decision to avoid utilitarian choices? On what grounds?

The form of this problem is important. Utilitarian modes com-pletely dominate business strategy formation and the organizational design of businesses. Success in these things is always judged against narrow and utilitarian measures of performance. The great and continual upheavals of decisions in these domains continually wreck the bases for building trust. Trust has no stable climate within which to develop. This is not deliberate (usually) but is probably intentional at a subconscious level. There is much shame for decision makers in seeing their achievements eclipsed by people who do not even see their work as relevant.

For trust is necessarily formed relationship by relationship. It cannot be a programme, a reorganization or a revolution. It is what it is and it does what it does. It puts relationship first without making it the only thing. It works with the grain of human society without needing to appeal to external motivation and its attendant greed and fear.

So how can a change occur? This transition, in my experience, happens on a daily basis, though it is often disrupted. People find corp-orate cultures so parched and barren that they quite naturally form clusters of individuals who work to provide a more rewarding environ-ment for each other. These groups are not necessarily within a single organization. They naturally have no loyalty to the negatives that spawned them. What they focus on and work towards bears no allegiance to the pay and other resources provided for them. They exist because what these people are supposed to be doing is pointless.

Where groups of people remain tolerated or unnoticed, a fascin-ating symbiosis appears. Organizations need the power and vision of such groups. Such structures often get labelled something to do with innovation, skunk-works and super-teams. The trust within the group can remain intact so long as the organizations involved know how to stay at arm's length and not introduce contradictions such as imposed goals and measures.

This creates a sort of trust-at-one-remove. These groups are treated as different, and so long as they deliver things that the organization wants but cannot get elsewhere they may be tolerated. Where there is a major external challenge to be met, such groups may well be involved and may meet up with other groups in other organizations – perhaps in a supply-chain initiative. Such agglomeration of groups that are in some way outsiders is fairly explosive because of their increasing power vis-à-vis the control needs of the organizations concerned.

Top-Down Models

There is a growing list of situations where there is a business case available, based on trust, that is not accessible via the existing cultures. I have worked on several multi-application smartcard schemes where this was the case and it often applies in supply chains and their ability to deliver integrity, for instance in food safety or in multi-modal transport.

In these cases the business logic is reversed:

- the business is only sensibly available via business structures based on trust;
- the existing management arrangements have to be assessed, principally to make sure that they do not act to counter trust;
- the new structures need to emphasize the development of new sources of value;
- each partner in the scheme needs to ask who they need to trust about what (information sharing, service provision, risk management, joint customer offerings) and work to develop the necessary trust.

The Heathrow Express Rail Link

One of the standard case studies is the Heathrow Express rail link. This was run as a conventional construction project, meaning man-to-man marking across all contractual boundaries and institutionalized suspicion of all claims. The culture contributed directly to the collapse of a tunnel underneath the airport, which threatened the prime goal of the project: not to disrupt airport operations. Surprisingly, top management at BAA and the contractors took the lesson on board and realized that the only way to get the project back on schedule was to develop a partnership approach. The team was stripped down to contain only people directly involved in productive work and communications among the team fostered and supported by a team of consultants, who focused on culture and ingrained adversarial practices. In the result the project was turned from disaster to success. Once again, however, the good practice was not immediately adopted elsewhere.

We can usefully note some of the other features of the project:

- Such was the distrust of the rest of the rail network that trains and systems were deliberately made so as not to allow interoperation with the national network.
- The investigation by the HSE into the tunnelling method involved in the accident contributed to delay in building the Jubilee Line Extension to the London Underground, which project suffered massive time and cost overruns despite a highly public commitment to toughness, accountability and the best project management.

'Not a day late' was the early watchword.

Trust Is Self-Reinforcing

Teams who trust each other know what they can achieve that other people cannot. People who don't want to or don't know how to put relationships before individual advantage know that teamwork is a chimera, a fantasy played out by people who are not rational about where their true interests lie.

What counts as observation and evidence is completely dependent on your starting assumptions. This is no surprise: most knowledge and a great deal of 'science' is actually self-fulfilling of the reasons given (or remaining covert) for investigation. This is why the impressive results of trust do not get generalized as a lesson, and equally why people whose inclination is to trust cannot empathize with those stuck in individualistic competitiveness.

So trust is self-confirming, self-reinforcing, self-rewarding and unless it is destroyed from the outside will persist and strengthen. The tragedy, as we have explored at length, is that the view of motivation held in most business cultures does act directly to destroy trust. We can catalogue some of these by way of summary:

(1) All systems of measures and targets imply an external motivation and an external definition of what 'should' be done that asserts itself above and against the internal motivation of trust. This comment applies equally to 'team' motivation schemes.

(2) All systems of norms and rules, all mandatory processes and procedures if they are thought to be absolute and non-negotiable in practice will conflict with the local and particular demands of trust. However, flexibly construed processes can be a huge support for trust.

(3) All notions of authority based in hierarchy and position or office are inimical to trust between people in the system. Authentic trust is explicitly replaced with and displaced by authority trust. And for teams, network trust is similarly displaced by commodity trust.

(4) All abstract notions such as consensus and voting, by their nature do not respect or even perceive individual relationships and the value of trust in them. All notions of consultation based on the idea of individual preferences and views work to undermine the joint 'we' of relationship and team.

(5) All relationships that are seductive in promising things they cannot deliver undermine the ability to form relationships that have integrity and that can build trust.

16

Working with Trust, Power and Risk

Insights and strategies for business success are quickly nullified by typical business cultures. Even glaring opportunities to improve go begging as we saw above. In fact, typical business cultures are precisely social mechanisms for resisting all sorts of change. But we cannot end a book on the application of trust in business without an attempt at a straightforward 'this is how you make progress'.

Peddling Solutions

Now, the first hurdle in seeing how to apply trust involves cutting through the huge number of 'solutions' that are pressing in on us. 'Applying trust', though, is not a solution; it is closer to being a question – a move that will open things up rather than close them down or control them. It is a move towards having degrees of freedom and that implies new risk and a new sort of power – the power to make decisions that change the game.

From the perspective of trust, all the solutions that people press forwards are actually manifestations of problems belonging to the suppliers of those solutions. It is not that we need the solution, it is that they need to sell it to us. The World Bank needs poverty more than poverty needs the World Bank. It is no wonder that solutions do not solve anything. All they do is connect us in ever more complex ways with problems that were not part of the original problem. Solutions are attractive because they purport to do magic: they purport to get us past the heart of the problem in the key relationships involved without having to engage in vulnerable negotiations.

So the process of changing trust from an intangible abstraction into a positive influence on real-world behaviour begins with getting a true understanding of what we are faced with.

Scimitar Risk Management System

When we have a clear idea of what we want to achieve – a vision, a goal, an objective – Scimitar gives us a powerful and effective way of identifying and dealing with things that could prevent us doing so. Scimitar began life in response to the simple and urgent question:

> Why do so many change initiatives not work out the way people thought they would?

In labelling and describing it as a risk 'management' system, though, we run foul of the way our language works. Essentially, Scimitar is about optimizing – getting the very best out of – the position we are in. However, in English common usage (a trusted commodity the world over), optimization implies second-best, a compromise, a settling for something that is acceptable. In a business context, on top of that it carries with it connotations of stopwatches, time and motion studies, and yesterday's O&M departments. We get all this when we hear 'optimum' whereas the word really means most favourable. 'Management', too, has its drawback in this context, given that it implies controlling.

Risk and trust, as we have seen, are organic and interconnected. They change with context. And the idea that they can be controlled leads us to hubris (and heartbreak). So if Scimitar is not allowed to 'optimize' and cannot 'manage', what exactly does it do? The answer is that it 'husbands' – makes best economic use of – the opportunities facing us. Words are important, the fact that it works brilliantly, more so.

Scimitar works by dynamically balancing all the competing influences at play in the situation that has to be husbanded (OK, managed). It is drill-down because the influences themselves comprise

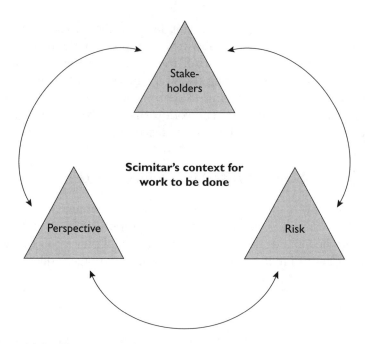

Figure 16.1   The context of work in Scimitar

influences *ad infinitum* that also have to be balanced, and it is iterative because the landscape changes as influences are addressed. It uses
triangles to capture the sense of these dynamics. Within Scimitar,
balancing implies building relationships that support negotiating for
desired outcomes.

At its highest – macro – level, it begins with a context model of
the territory to be managed. At its lowest – micro – level, it comprises
the packets of work that have to be done to deliver the plan. Between
the two is a system of managing, the POSIWID of which is business
improvement.

What is important as far as our work in this book is concerned is
to show clearly how Scimitar takes seemingly abstract ideas about
trust and turns them into packets of real-world work that can change
things. A high-level look at the way it works will suffice. It begins
by setting the context, taking a helicopter view (Figure 16.1).

Scimitar's macro context is bounded by business perspective,
stakeholders and risks. These are drilled-down into below. For now,
though, this is what the dimensions of the macro picture comprise:

- *Perspective* reflects and balances the organization's vision, its skill-base and its values.
- *Risk* identifies where there is a lack of control, a lack of information or a lack of time.
- *Stakeholders* are people with whom realistic negotiations can be held to begin managing risks. To qualify as stakeholders people must have power to do something about them, they must be proximate to where the risk will strike and they must have some interest (within the financial meaning of the word) in getting the risk addressed.

With this context drawn up and agreed, and with stakeholder and risk databases in place, the work can begin.

Very often the first issue Scimitar highlights is a lack of stakeholders. People are often reluctant to acknowledge their power, proximity and interest or else their immediate concerns that preclude their engagement with the challenge. Engaging stakeholders is frequently the very first real task risk managers face. Often there is even denial that the risks exist or are in any way real. This is an easy and logical outcome when people go to a network trust place where 'us' and 'them' are clearly identifiable. All risk is perceived as emanating from 'them'.

That said, a brief drill-down of Scimitar looks like Figure 16.2.

Perspective

In the perspective diagram (Figure 16.2), we look at a space bounded by:

- typical business concerns of vision, the market and business strategy;
- typical work concerns of skills, experience, tools and training;
- typical people concerns of trust, authenticity, authority and values.

By balancing these concerns in looking at a particular problem, we gain an accurate workable perspective reflecting our awareness, resourcefulness and energy. Conversely, if we have an unbalanced perspective – say, we overemphasize, for instance, the ability of an improved business vision to bring control – then we are likely to

Perspective

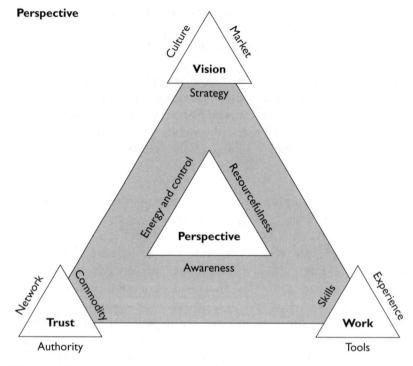

Figure 16.2 Balancing vision, work and trust to get perspective

struggle. (People like using this diagram because it links concerns that are rarely dealt with in a unified way and attaches real solutions to them.)

So we look at problems and proposed solutions in terms of where they fit in this space. What sort of a problem are we looking at? What sorts of solutions are we looking at? Do we assume this is a question of understanding the market or of training our sales people? Do we assume that people can bring themselves to this sales task or might their integrity be being compromised? What is the relationship between the salesperson's sense of integrity and our understanding of the market? What would the effect of training be on these questions? What is our training provider's view of these issues? What is their level of commitment?

Very often we see technical solutions proposed to problems of business focus and organizational coherence. Can this ever make sense? The solutions put forward speak to a denial of the original problem and a need to be seen to be doing something. From this perspective, the question of who needs to be trusted about what, the central question of any trust strategy, will be extremely obscure.

Notice that each corner of our perspective space has a different focus but still needs trust. Authenticity (best thought of as a person's capacity to put as much of herself or himself into the work as possible) most obviously requires space for people to be themselves. But the development of business vision and strategy is equally a matter of trust if anyone is to commit to it. By the same token, so is understanding the market. The development of skills and experience is of no use without the trust to allow their application to the problem, to do real work and to head off prisoners' dilemmas.

Stakeholding

Having begun our analysis (and simultaneous integration) we need to move to understanding the social web. Who are the stakeholders we must concern ourselves with and what is their position with regard to the problem? We characterize stakeholding in terms of power, proximity and interest (Figure 16.3).

The power of stakeholders is their ability to act to influence a situation for good or for ill. Their proximity is their necessary involvement with the situation because of their role or their investment in the issues. Interest refers both to the degree to which the situation engages the attention of the stakeholder and to interest in the sense of how much skin they have in the game. These are difficult to distinguish in practice.

Stakeholder management involves the realignment of the power, proximity and interest of the set of stakeholders to allow constructive action. From the perspective of trust, the helicopter view implied in the previous sentence is not available and the job is to work out where to place trust to unlock the potential of the situation: to get the positive engagement of key stakeholders and to generate the energy to take things forward without needing to push.

Since trust is not an automatic choice for a relationship strategy, we need to get to a position where we trust the stakeholders we most need to work with and somehow work round or marginalize the stakeholders

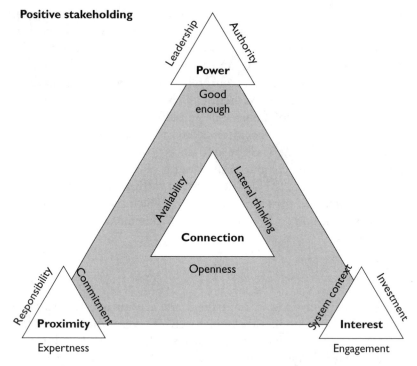

Figure 16.3 Connection comes from power, proximity and interest

who are really not people we can engage with. In the latter category must come people, for instance, whose instinct is to use trust to their own advantage, irrespective of the damage to relationships that follows. The stakeholders who remain outside authentic trust need to be placed within hierarchical, commodity or network trust orbits as seems appropriate.

As a brief excursion, we can look at the shadow side of stakeholding to see the symptoms of situations where people default to negative uses of power (Figure 16.4). In our experience these are very common. The reason for taking the risk of trust is often to break into these self-defeating modes and challenge people to deal with the real issues.

So the shadow side of power is hubris, the shadow side of interest is abdication and that of proximity is seduction. We have labelled the central triangle as focus, because the busy-ness, defensiveness and disconnection that usually accompany a single-minded focus describe

Shadow-side stakeholding

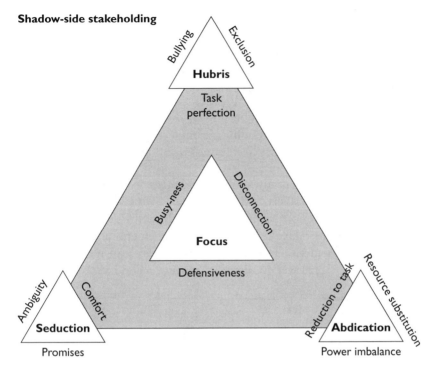

Figure 16.4 A blinkered focus comes from hubris, seduction and abdication

the underbelly of organizational life. This is the territory of the 'jobsworth' and the middle managers who have learnt by painful experience to keep their noses clean. Everything that a stakeholder can do can get pulled into the shadow-side logic that avoids all engagement with the real work. By contrast, positive stakeholding gives openness and availability, a connection with the issues and an understanding that interdependence exists and that choices must be made.

When we boil the challenge of trust right down to its essentials we get another triangle: trust, risk and awareness (Figure 16.5). Trust implies taking radical risks and is not really trust unless we are aware of the situation and how those risks will play out. The risks we need to take in business are in dealing with others in a way that allows business projects to be successful: we need to trust people to bring out their contribution and we need to be aware of how the situation could have different dynamics if we did. We need to be aware of a situation and our role in it without rushing into action and without projecting our issues onto others. We need to trust ourselves both to act and to remain quiet, and we need to be ready to take the risks without which we cannot generate the possibilities for success.

It is challenging to trust people because they can let us down and betray us. The risk we take is:

- psychic in terms of our belief in our own judgement;
- social in terms of our standing among our peers;
- commercial in terms of the business assets we can lose.

In reality, those risks are always there, whether we consider the issues of trust or not. By actively taking these risks, we make them manageable for the first time. Our awareness of the nature of the risks and how they work is developed by our engagement and our active, practical involvement. The trinity of trust, risk and awareness give us positive power, power to discover, power to build social resources.

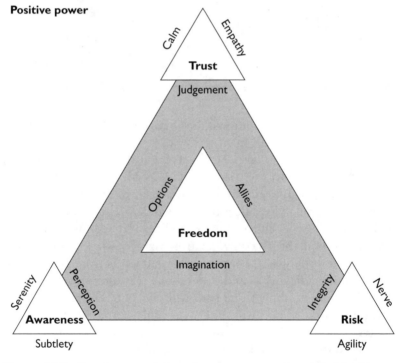

Figure 16.5 Freedom to act flows from trust, awareness and risk-taking

To go back to the notion of solutions, we can now see the risk that solutions purport to be able to avoid. It goes something like this:

We don't have to expose ourselves to this danger, we can use something that someone else has done, a proven way to get the results we need without the risk. We do not have to trust people, we can have commodity trust in the product or service and we can have a contract to protect our interests in law.

For all important problems, this is a piece of seduction by the supplier. Seduction is making promises that have no way of being kept. For the promises to be real there would need to be a different level of engagement between supplier and customer, a different attitude on both sides and an understanding of the trust equations.

To go back to our simple, how-to process, we are exploring which stakeholders we have to trust and which risks we have to take. We need

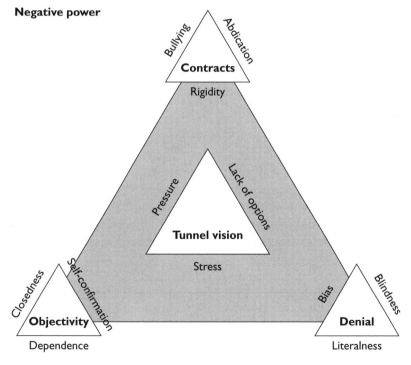

Figure 16.6 Contractual mindsets, an insistence on objectivity and denial result in tunnel vision

to sort out which risks are intrinsic and which can be avoided. Again, it may help us to see what the shadow side looks like (Figure 16.6).

Contracts, 'objectivity' and denial are all designed to remove challenge and bring comfort and safety. Much of this book has been devoted to challenging the notion that there is any safety and comfort at all to be had via these mechanisms, but they are still standard fare. They work to push the formal 'should be' aspects of a situation to the foreground and the real 'anomaly' aspects to the background, away from awareness. We end up dealing with what it is acceptable to see. We buy solutions that reinforce our prejudices. We try to export the risk that reality is not as we see it.

So our process moves to ask:

- What do we need to be most keenly aware of in order to succeed?
- Who do we need to trust to develop that awareness – which stakeholders, which experts, which entrepreneurial explorers?
- What risks does that trust open up and how do those risks sharpen our awareness?

There is a positive cycle available, and it is the functioning of this positive cycle that tells us we are on the right track. If we manage (and we may well fail – we do not exercise arbitrary power) to move around the cycle we will develop positive power. If we shortcut the loop our power will immediately move into negative modes that interfere with the potential for success. There are always local and suboptimal successes to distract and waylay our progress. All stakeholders are able to improve their lot in the short term by selling out. The bond of trust is what makes progress possible and the strength of the bond is our only guarantee. And yet the bond is almost universally neglected as a strategic issue.

Conclusions: The Necessity of Risk and the Shadow Side

We have come on a long and somewhat scattered journey through different sorts of trust and the roles they play in our business world. We have emphasized throughout the positive nature of taking risks, especially of taking the risk of trust to bring the talents of others to bear on the problems we face. Our final points relate to the role of risk and the shadow side in grounding and energizing everything we do.

Why don't we just trust people? Well, it feels risky to do so and we have been taught to exercise prudence and caution in our business dealings. Why should it feel risky and why should we be cautious? Well, we need to because people will betray us and take advantage of our trust if we are not careful. Why would people act in that way? Well, there is always a short-term and local advantage to be had, and sometimes the shadow-side game spreads to engulf whole sectors and industries.

So to create the businesses we want and to build a positive culture that can resist shadow-side effects, we need to take risks. The shadow side is the context and the driver for those risks. If we don't take the risk of trust we are, *de facto*, pulled into shadow-side dynamics with all that that implies. These are two sides of a coin: we take the low-risk, low-gain road or we take the high-risk, high-gain road. The low road embeds us in games in which we betray and manipulate each other and use our power negatively. The high road uses the energy we gain from escaping those games to build better ways to do business.

Without experiencing the shadow side, we do not know the risks we run and we do not understand the privilege of managing those risks for each other. Without acknowledging the shadow side, we cannot draw on the energy for change that it can bring. To deny the shadow side is to be pulled into its power, it is whistling in the dark rather than switching the light on. It is the general denial of the effect that business cultures have on the people who work in them that gives such opportunity to people who want to subvert them for their own ends.

So trust is only necessary and only difficult because of the cultures we have built. Very few business people I have worked with are able to take responsibility for, and ownership of, the cultures they work in and with. Culture-change programmes are almost always about them rather than about us, always about making people more malleable rather than having more integrity and more ability to resist shadow-side games.

In the end it is always about where you want to get to. We are far too ready to scope down our ambitions and to focus on concrete things and the bottom line. This leaves 95% of what needs to be paid attention to unmanaged. Remember:

- only a vision can be at risk;
- only risks you actively decide to take can be managed;
- only trust will allow other people to help;
- any other sort of power is tainted.

The Anatomy of a Fall from Trust

There is a common pattern to many trust failures that takes us on a tour around the four types of trust. It is worth rehearsing and it is worth remembering because it illustrates the serial mistakes that are possible when the difference between the different sorts of trust is not understood.

The original failure is usually in customer relationships and commodity trust. The company believes in its products and believes that the customer only wants a good product: there is nothing else to do. This relationship deficit is unstable, as we have pointed out before. The whole weight of continued commercial trading rests on customer satisfaction with the product, which is to say that when the product is no longer satisfactory, for whatever reason, real or imaginary, then trading takes a dive.

The second failure is the failure to see that the product or the customer interest is changing. This is a very short step from the first failure. Perhaps the actions of a pressure group, possibly some revelations on a television documentary, a shift in fashion or an undetected change in the input materials for the product and suddenly (so it seems) the successful product is no longer successful. The proposition underlying commodity trust that the consumers' interests are being taken care of is suddenly perceived to be false.

Now commodity trust is delivered by managed systems. Internally in the producing organization, people know that it is their system of controls that delivers a consistent product. So typically the third mistake is to go to a place of authority trust and say 'we know our product is as good as ever' or 'our systems will take care of the changing circumstances'. But of course to say this is to say 'we are the experts, we know what is good for you' which is to say 'Mr

Consumer, you are wrong'. This is both an easy and a ridiculous step. Of course producers relying on commodity trust do actually feel that their customers are stupid. This is a very common topic of conversation. But it throws into relief the proposition that consumers are expected to buy the product because the producer knows it is the right choice. Oh dear.

Of course, the consumers have already moved to a network trust place. They are discussing the fall from trust with all and sundry, and it is in the gossip columns and the subject of radio chat. This is clearly a job for PR and the spokesmen and women are rolled out to speak smooth words and point out that plenty of people are still buying the product because they are not swayed by the surface froth and trivia. A battle for hearts and minds ensues, albeit weighed down by the leaden-footed early moves. But this is the fourth failure: it becomes clear that a battle for hearts and minds is taking place and that the producer will say whatever it takes to get people back on side. Consumers get cynical – 'Well, they would say that, wouldn't they?' There are no facts available because the credibility of the producer's authority has already been trashed by using it to say the consumer is wrong.

In the end it often comes to a showdown. The chairman is wheeled out. He has very few options. He can take the blame as a scapegoat and go. He can battle on and hope he is respected for doing so and that better times are around the corner. Or he can eat humble pie and say that under his guidance the company lost sight of being in business for the benefit of customers. His problems stem from the fact that he has no trust resources to work from and that he is under the spotlight, a place of maximum publicness. He has to somehow make up for the unwillingness and inability of his company to deal with customers as people. So the final failure is the failure to generate an authentic response at the last ditch. At this point consumers want to see if they have been dealing with a company led by a human or a business automaton.

A Better Way?

Lots of companies do it better, basically by building relationship and credibility before they need it. This, of course, is already an acknowledgement that stakeholders of all kinds have minds of their own and owe no *prima facie* allegiance to a company just because it is there. The problems we have illustrated are perhaps clearest around companies that do think they have a permanent place – the utilities and the monopoly providers, the quangos and politically sponsored businesses.

As with any emergency procedure, there is no need to wait for the real fire to see if the company can generate an authentic response to customer concerns. The only problem with practices and fire drills is that the cutting edge can be missing, leading to the commoditization of the necessary attitudes and skills. It takes real leadership to actually take on board what customers think and to reconnect company actions with customer concerns. But it is the tiny individual actions, trivial in themselves, that build the capital of trust that allows recovery in bad times.

We can go one step deeper into this. If I pay attention to keeping my options open, keeping real degrees of freedom, then the trust types look like this:

- Authentic trust *is* choice: it represents complete freedom to act.
- Network trust is inconsistent and many-faceted. I can choose who to believe and who to doubt, and there will always be someone who can understand my point of view and connect it into other concerns. So network trust constrains my degrees of freedom but not significantly.
- Authority trust used in older models of society used to be non-negotiable, but today I am as likely to doubt authority because it is authority and because of its own constraints of publicness as I am to trust in what I am told. So authority can be repressive still and aspects of trust can be forced on me, but this too is not a big problem.
- But commodity trust is take-it-or-leave-it. It is non-negotiable. You either buy a product or you don't. For a commodity you never get to influence what you buy. It is a *cul-de-sac*. There is no way out short of refusing commodity trust and rejecting the product. Sometimes it isn't even practical to reject the product: I am using Windows as I write, after all. Somehow it is natural that our hugely vaunted consumer freedom, lifestyle, standard of living is actually the place of our bondage and our lack of any significant choice.

It is, of course, precisely this sense of bondage and lack of options that fuels the periodic consumer revolt whose pattern we have traced above. The politics of uncertainty sees the difficulties and doubt generated by 'solutions' pushed down onto the powerless until they reject the whole concept. To get past this revolt, companies need to deal with all the 'side effects' their solutions unwittingly generate: they need to feel the customer experience in some authentic way.

We have described these effects largely from a consumer perspective. They are more complex but arguably more important in a business-to-business setting. Many companies manage a token social conscience with respect to the public but think that businesses need to be able to survive in the corporate jungle and that paying authentic attention to them is misplaced. We disagree.

Annotated Bibliography

Some books are covered below in the section on 'Gurus you can trust' rather than in the bibliographic list for the book, to avoid duplication.

Francis Fukuyama, *Trust: The Social Virtues and the Creation of Prosperity*, New York: Free Press, 1995

Fukuyama deals with trust as a parameter that differs between cultures and societies, and is able to trace effects from cultural features of micro-economies to their macro-economic effects. Although Fukuyama never really argues about what trust is and how it works, his insights on the close mapping of patterns and spans of trust to economic style and the sizes of organizations that are viable extends our argument into the macro-economic sphere.

Rita Cruise O'Brien, *Trust: Releasing the Energy to Succeed*, Chichester: John Wiley & Sons, 2001

O'Brien takes an almost ethnographic approach to the study of some high performing teams in assessing the role of trust in their performance. She ultimately has a recipe-based approach to generating trust in others: we cannot follow down this road. There is a wealth of case material and energetic interpretation here that will suit more action oriented and less philosophical readers.

Thomas Webler, Eugene A. Rosa, Carlo C. Jaeger and Ortwin
   Renn, *Risk, Uncertainty, and Rational Action*, London:
   Earthscan, 2001

A survey of the connections between how we conceive of uncertainty in technology and environment and the implication of that
for business policy and what we consider to be rational. Businesses
have been less skilled than society in general at understanding risks
that go beyond what can be calculated and what can be controlled.
It is as though businesses can only deal with things they perceive to
be within their sphere of competence.

Ulrich Beck, *Risk Society: Towards a New Modernity*, Newbury Park,
   CA: Sage, 1992

Beck is an eminent sociologist who has studied the way society and
its institutions deal with risks they cannot quantify or control. He
shows the absurdity of much that passes for risk management mechanism, such as the villages being poisoned by pollution from adjacent
glass factories which cannot be sued because no one can prove which
factory fatal pollution came from. He shows how institutions fall apart
in terms of the authority of their pronouncements in the face of major
disasters such as the fallout from Chernobyl.

Peter Marris, *The Politics of Uncertainty: Attachment in Private and
   Public Life*, London: Routledge, 1996

Marris deals with a set of sociological concerns about what happens
when you use power to push uncertainty onto others. One of the
features of political and social life is that people do not go away when
they are disenfranchised and made to carry a disproportionate share
of social burdens. We show how to apply these insights in business
environments and how the structures of trust affect the usual
dynamics.

Bruce Schneier, *Secrets and Lies: Digital Security in a Networked
   World*, New York: John Wiley & Sons, 2000

Schneier starts with people's beliefs about computer security and
shows that an altogether different approach is needed. He shows that
security is about understanding threats and patterns of trust, not about

systems engineering. One of the strengths of Bruce's book and his style is to debunk the idea that the big players are competent. My favourite story is about the USA selling banknote printing presses to the Shah of Iran and then being unable to prevent millions of authentic dollar notes being printed by the revolutionary regime after the fall of the Shah.

Dennis Reina and Michelle Reina, *Trust and Betrayal in the Workplace: Building Effective Relationships in Your Organization*, San Francisco, CA: Berrett-Koehler, 1999

The Reinas deal with HR issues inside organizations, and have a view of trust that is really more about the absence of mistrust. They take the view that an organization is effective and is sometimes undermined by mistrust. Our view is that organizations are riddled with mistrust and that trust is a radical strategy for doing business. There is practical advice here for people who do not want to rock the boat.

Geoff Mulgan, *Connexity: How to Live in a Connected World*, London: Chatto & Windus, 1997

Mulgan's concerns are largely with public policy and the effect of increasing interdependence on the assumptions behind current policies. He is very optimistic about outcomes. Our viewpoint is both more pragmatically business-centred and more pessimistic about what we will all have to understand and to deal with. Essentially Mulgan raises questions about the relationship between connexity and democratic politics and draws hope from the increasing interconnection of citizens for the democratic processes. We think this hope is misplaced unless people can understand the leap of faith that is required to build trust and engagement.

Karl Weick, *Sensemaking in Organizations*, Thousand Oaks, CA: Sage, 1995

Weick's concern is to show how we go about constructing meanings in organizations and how situated and contingent those meanings are. Our concern is to apply the patterns of meaning-making across multiple organizations and to understanding the structures that can underpin trust. Weick is seminal in showing how multiple meanings

are always available and the sorts of social processes that lead to particular meanings coming to dominate.

L. Jean Camp, *Trust and Risk in Internet Commerce*, Cambridge, MA: MIT Press, 2000

Camp takes a monetary and informational view on trust and risk and does not consider human relationships. She is concerned to translate between technical protocol and financial risk. Our concern is to translate a second time into the way these issues affect business relationships and willingness to do business.

Richard Veryard, *The Component-Based Business: Plug and Play*, London: Springer-Verlag, 2001

Veryard analyses how the properties of components at a business level can describe what happens when new businesses are created by assembling them. Veryard exposes the business concerns that are often glossed over in the rush to be first to market. Veryard is a close colleague of ours and our concerns are in many ways complementary to his, focusing on the organizational aspects while he focuses on the role of technology.

Gurus You Can Trust with Ideas You Can Use

We can describe the essence of a guru as an ability to surprise. A guru gets people to enlighten themselves by connecting what they already know with what they think they do not know. A guru is never a commodity whose ideas you have to take on trust, because the ideas are alive in evoking knowledge or they are nothing.

Here are the gurus we use and the ones you may enjoy. They are capable of illuminating the trust ideas in the book.

Albert Borgmann
Makes clear the extent to which commodity trust rules our lives. Explaining why we like the Marlboro Man despite ourselves (he lives in Montana by the way, so he and Marlboro Man are neighbours), Borgmann leaves us in absolutely no doubt that Marlboro Country is actually a cemetery. The medium is the message written on a gravestone.

In his work on what he calls the structure of information, he identifies three layers: natural information he describes as information *about* reality; cultural information he describes as information *for* reality; and technological information he describes as information *as* reality. The technological layer overrides the other two so that 'computers' are the only truth. The medium is the message in binary code.

Technology and the Character of Contemporary Life: A Philosophical Enquiry, Chicago, IL: University of Chicago Press, 1984

Crossing the Postmodern Divide, Chicago, IL: University of Chicago Press, 1993

Holding on to Reality: The Nature of Information at the Turn of the Millennium, Chicago, IL: University of Chicago Press, 1999

Albert Einstein (1879–1955)

Reckoned imagination is more important than knowledge. And who am I to argue? 'Knowledge,' he said, 'is limited whereas imagination encircles the world'. So rather than merely taking the tram, he imagined he was riding on a beam of light to the office. He got off at the stop where $E = mc^2$, changed the world and ushered in a new age.

Ideas and Opinions, New York: Random House, 1988

The World as I See It, New York: Carol, 1993

Bernard Williams (b1929)

Brilliant academic and moral philosopher who reckons we're all capable of making significant discoveries through reflection and reasoning. But only when we *think straight about things*. Too often, though, he reckons we're better at conclusions than we are at reasons. As often as not this is because we surround any good stuff we have with rotten thinking. Publicness is rotten thinking. That's a great trust message.

'Formal Structures and Social Reality', in Gambetta, Diego (ed.) *Trust: Making and Breaking Cooperative Relations*, electronic edition, Dept of Sociology, University of Oxford, chapter 1, pp 3–13, http://www.sociology.ox.ac.uk/papers/williams3–13.doc

Truth and Truthfulness: An Essay in Genealogy, Princeton, NJ: Princeton University Press, 2002

Plato (428–347 Before the common era)
Responsible for probably the world's earliest example of the medium being the message. In *The Republic* he tells the story of a cave in which the inhabitants of a dark subterranean place live under the delusion that shadows of cut-outs passing before them are the real world. They dread not having their delusions. There's no better description anywhere of life in the bottom left-hand corner of our trust model.

The Republic, Benjamin Jowett (trans), New York: Vintage Books, 1991

Fernando Flores (b 1941)
The inventor of transformation through assessment, Flores's main message is that the language of truth requires trust. By way of illustrating this, he picks out what he calls 'speech acts' – language rituals that build trust, which then become the beginnings of the transformation process.

The need for transformation, he reckons, never arises because we don't understand 'business' but because we don't understand people. The reason for this is that we spend practically all our lives concerned with things we know and things we don't know – the place where Machiavelli's 'present necessities' dominate our lives. Transformation can only happen when we concern ourselves with things we don't know we don't know. By way of driving the hard message of trust, he tells us that hope is the raw material of losers.

Robert C. Solomon and Fernando Flores, *Building Trust: in Business, Politics, Relationships and Life*, Oxford: Oxford University Press, 2001

Charles Spinosa, Hubert L. Dreyfus and Fernando Flores, *Disclosing New Worlds: Entrepreneurship, Democratic Action, and the Cultivation of Solidarity*, Cambridge, MA: MIT Press, 1999

Fred Herzberg (1923–2000)
The absolute genuine article when it comes to motivation, and the inventor of 'job enrichment'. Herzberg's hygiene-motivation theory has still to be bettered for its simplicity, power, applicability and its contribution to productivity. His case that hygiene factors alone can never motivate us whereas their absence demotivates us absolutely, is one of management's greatest insights. (We know this because it has become part of the conventional wisdom and as such is easily

ignored. And only powerful stuff gets treated this badly and survives.) Transposed to the trust arena, the hygiene model works equally brilliantly. This is because the heart of motivation and the heart of authentic trust come together in Herzberg's immortal words: *treat me as I am, not as you want me to be.*

Herzberg on Motivation, Cleveland, OH: Penton Education, 1991

Slavoj Zizek (b 1949)
As far as authority and roles are concerned, we all 'become' the stories we tell about ourselves. Any manager feeling tempted to implement business improvements by finding ways to encourage his people to 'enjoy' things they are currently 'required' to do, should read Zizek first. By explaining – in a quirky, post-modern way that so far hasn't penetrated management books – how social systems learn to absorb change and re-regulate themselves, he lets us into a world where we can kid ourselves there are choices when in fact there aren't. 'We know what we're doing, but we do it anyway,' Zizek tells us. And we all know that risks can only be managed once they've been taken.

In the Bernard Williams four-box model we used to develop our trust model, we used Zizek's dimensions of consistent/inconsistent and authentic/inauthentic motivations as an overlay/alternative to those of Williams himself. This provided us with a useful way of validating the model.

Judith Butler, Slavoj Zizek and Ernesto Laclau, *Contingency, Hegemony, Universality: Contemporary Dialogues on the Left*, London: Verso, 2000

Did Somebody Say Totalitarianism?, London: Verso, 2001

Karl Marx (1818–1883)
Practically the whole of twentieth-century history attests to the power of his ideas. Some undeniably good work remains misunderstood and misinterpreted, with trust relationships remaining fatally damaged as a result. That's not to say that all his ideas have been dismissed as class-war polemic or similarly ridiculed by conventional wisdom: 'City Fat Cats', for example, ascribe readily to his labour theory of value when it comes to setting their 'compensation' packages. Thus, reification, as Marx described it, pertinently remains a determining characteristic of modern life. How else would you recognize a 'City Fat Cat' or his 'compensation' package?

Karl Marx and Friedrich Engels, *The Marx–Engels Reader*, Robert C. Tucker (ed.), New York: Norton, 1978

Groucho Marx (1890–1977)
Famous for 'not wishing to belong to a club that would accept him as a member' – which, however you choose to interpret it, represents a profound insight into the workings of network trust – Groucho practically perfected the art of disguising a deep truth as a one-liner. For example, '"military intelligence" is a contradiction of terms' resonates with the constraints imposed by authority trust.

Paraphrasing his view of politicians reveals a truth close to home: 'management has perfected the art of looking for trouble, finding it, misdiagnosing it and then applying the wrong remedies'. As the great man said himself, quote me as saying I was misquoted.

The Essential Groucho: Writings by, for, and about Groucho Marx, New York: Vintage Books, 2000

Antonio Genovesi (1712–1769)
Besides being the world's first professor of business and introducing Italy to the philosophical ideas of his contemporaries, he realigned the business curriculum to take account of the developments of the industrial revolution. Most importantly, though, in trust terms, Genovesi wrote and published in Italian. In doing so he broke the commodity trust stranglehold of Latin as the language of learning.

Thomas N. Bisson, *The Medieval Crown of Aragon: A Short History*, Oxford: Oxford University Press, 1991

Niccoló Machiavelli (1467–1527)
The idea that people are so ready to obey what they see as their 'present necessities' that anyone setting out to deceive will always find there are sufficient people willing to be deceived, is at the core of what today we call Machiavellianism. If you can actually set the 'present necessities' agenda, then so much the simpler. As a principle it's something we all learn quite shortly after our elevation to management. Like any manager, Machiavelli was in the business of delivering results, in his case for the benefit of the rulers of Renaissance Florence. He used the aforementioned principle with almost total success, effortlessly and regardless of whether the ends came to be considered good or bad. In trust terms, publicness is often little more than

humbug. Machiavelli saw this completely and documented ways in which it could be manipulated to whatever ends were required. His intellectual honesty about political dishonesty – prophets with guns, he reckons, will always beat prophets without guns – was at the heart of his success. It remains his enduring threat to hypocrisy in all its guises.

Michael A. Ledeen, *Machiavelli on Modern Leadership: Why Machiavelli's Iron Rules are as Timely and Important Today as Five Centuries Ago*, New York: Truman Talley, 2000

Tom Paine (1737–1809)

Three all-time great books were published in the year 1776. Adam Smith's *The Wealth of Nations*, Edward Gibbon's *History of the Decline and Fall of the Roman Empire* and Tom Paine's *Common Sense*. Smith's book began the academic study of economics, Gibbon's book defined the worldview for western democracies and Paine's book coined the term and led to the birth of the United States of America. *Common Sense*, besides providing real-world management insight into the interpretation and trustworthiness of official figures and audit reports (pre-dating Enron and Arthur Andersen by two and a quarter centuries), takes as its start point the very essence of risk management: 'a long habit of not thinking a thing wrong gives it a superficial appearance of being right, and raises, at first, a formidable outcry in defence of custom'. Formidable indeed, common sense indeed.

Common Sense, Isaac Kramnick (ed.), Harmondsworth: Penguin, 1983

John Kenneth Galbraith (b1908)

Men who grow more liberal and freethinking with age are rare indeed. Great and influential thinkers who do so are rarer still. Galbraith, a self-confessed 'abiding liberal', is such a man. An agricultural economist by inclination and training, he headed the team sent by the US Congress to carry out an economic assessment of the war in Germany immediately hostilities ceased. While the trust and management implications of his findings are painfully revealing, the pressures put on him to ensure his report said the 'right things' were still more revealing. Not even the authenticity of Galbraith's report could stop the inevitable post-war development of the military–industrial complex, the building of the Pentagon and the spiralling growth of the US defence budget, the trust implications of which are being felt still at the time of writing. In fact, they are now the *conventional wisdom* – ideas so ingrained nobody ever questions them – the great man warned us about in his 1958 book, *The Affluent Society*, and for which we're still paying the price. Galbraith feels his greatest achievement was not his books but his time as head of the body responsible for US price controls during the Second World War. He contrasts the success of this with the inflation that took place after the First World War when the Fed was in charge. 'Historians never mention inflation as they did after World War One. *But if – and I think this is the rule of all public service – if you succeed your work is forgotten.*' (This poignant insight is the perfect corollary to Smith's Law; see entry for Keynes below.)

A Short History of Financial Euphoria, Harmondsworth: Penguin, 1994

The Affluent Society, Boston, MA: Houghton Mifflin, 1998

A Life in Our Times (autobiography), New York: Ballantine Books, 1982

John Maynard Keynes (1883–1946)
As the pre-eminent economist of his time – his General Theory of Employment, Interest and Money remains the outstanding guide to effective management of a liberal economy – Keynes was uniquely and definitively able to set out the economic costs and consequences of two world wars. Two trust implications of his work are significant. First, he established the public face of money once and for all by suspending the gold standard in 1931. Second, he was the central figure in rebuilding the post-war economy of the world – the Bretton Woods agreement of 1944.

Keynes contended that people like him, in situations like that, in order to do any good, must do things that are unorthodox, troublesome, dangerous and disobedient. Out of this a new instrument for adapting and controlling the working of economic forces was invented. The World Bank began life as a truly radical idea to counter deeply entrenched problems. Keynes died before his idea became reality and in the intervening fifty-odd years, the forces of conventional wisdom have entirely changed the bank's nature, so much so that today the bank gets far more out of poverty than poverty gets out of the bank. The bank's trust position slides ever closer to the bottom left-hand corner of the trust space and, with the inversion of trust, another great idea becomes reduced to a POSIWID that depends on the continued existence of the calamity it was designed to rid the world of. Where poverty is concerned, trust is nowhere. Exposure to the workings and culture of the World Bank led the authors to set out what they happily call Smith's Law:

> An organization cannot have a mission to solve a problem without being dependent on the problem remaining unsolved.

which generalizes to:

> An organization is engaged both in achieving its goals and in not achieving them: for every n people engaged directly in working towards a goal there are m others who are working to address the reasons why the goal cannot be achieved. There is permanent structural ambivalence about achieving any significant end. (See Galbraith's corollary.)

Essays in Persuasion, London: Macmillan, 1984

W. Edwards Deming (1900–1993)

Deming's life work comes down to us as the PDSA cycle – plan, do, study, act – and the startling insight that quality must be designed in, that it cannot be factored in after the event. As far as trust is concerned his crucial message is contained in the notion that the purpose of system is what it does – POSIWID rules – regardless of what the designers, builders, implementers, testers or anyone else intends.

Mary Walton, Foreword by W. Edwards Deming, *The Deming Management Method*, New York: Perigee, 1986

Rafael Aguayo, *Dr. Deming: The American Who Taught the Japanese about Quality*, New York: Simon & Schuster, 1991

Søren Kierkegaard (1813–1855)

Capturing the absolute torment and absence of trust in Kierkegaard's life is practically impossible. To begin with he was one of seven siblings who, from their earliest years were all told by their father that they would die before they reached the age of thirty-four in payment of their father's sins (thirty-four was the age of Jesus at the crucifixion). Five of them did. Søren, though, survived. Everything he learned immediately undermined everything else he knew so that grounding his knowledge in anything he was secure in was out of the question. Trust in such circumstances is almost impossible. Life's challenge for him was to 'become who you are' – authenticity in any language – and the rest of his life was taken up in that existential quest. In the end he summed up the only thing he became able to trust when he said 'God doesn't exist but He is real.' Apart from this crucial insight – lots of things in management are real but don't exist – Kierkegaard, much as Genovesi had done for Italian a century earlier, made his native language, in this case Danish, a trusted commodity for learning where it had previously been secondary to Latin and German. The irony is that the paper he fought so hard to be allowed to publish in Danish was his treatise on irony.

Patrick Gardiner, *Kierkegaard* Oxford: Oxford University Press, 2002

Paul Strathern, *Kierkegaard in 90 Minutes*, Chicago, IL: I. R. Dee, 1997

Barry Oshry
Oshry was one of the first to identify organizations as systems, the point being that, unlike, say, a machine, which can be tuned or governed or in which a part can be replaced, changing a system is an altogether different challenge. He has made a lifelong study of power and powerlessness within social systems. His 'dance of blind reflex' insights perfectly capture the power dynamics that keep organizations located unhealthily in the trust space. Power is at the heart of all relationships and most power relationships are asymmetric. Oshry's work shows how even the most unpromising disparities can be overcome.

Organizational Spasms: When a Stable Organization Meets an Unstable Environment, Boston, MA: Power & Systems Training, 1978

Seeing Systems: Unlocking the Mysteries of Organizational Life, San Francisco, CA: Berrett-Koehler, 1996

Martin Heidegger (1889–1976)
Like Machiavelli and Marx, Heidegger has had something of a bad press. His work on 'self' and 'selfhood' has been picked up and used by some pretty unsavoury groups over the years (serving as much as anything as a focus for the destructive power of network trust).

He reckoned that the extremes of human 'being' – the act and process of being as opposed to the human being the person – were the opposite ends of a continuum running from *publicness* to *authenticity*.

Publicness he described as a complete loss of self in conformance with imposed preconceptions, options and values. At the other end of the scale, *authenticity* represents the individual's ultimate freedom of choice and achievement. In terms of trust analysis – without going to the guru's nihilistic and existential extremes – this is the clearest statement of authentic trust that is available.

Magda King and John Llewelyn (eds), *A Guide to Heidegger's Being and Time*, Albany, NY: State University of New York Press, 2001

Joan Stanbaugh (trans), *Being and Time: A Translation of Sein und Zeit*, Albany, NY: State University of New York Press, 1996

Marshall McLuhan (1911–1980)

The original media guru and inventor of communication studies, McLuhan was once called the 'oracle of the electronic age'. In fact he is credited with coining the word media in the sense we use it today. His work and influence are ubiquitous. Management conventional wisdom owes its recognition of the need to think creatively about complex issues almost entirely to McLuhan.

McLuhan reckons change is a kind of dynamic continuum in which any attempt at introducing something new has to deal with four effects. He calls the first of these effects retrieval – everything new has elements of the old, what he calls drawings from the cultural inventory. The second effect he calls enhancement – new requirements are built in to address the issues driving the change and often, unconsidered or trivial aspects of the previous regime are brought to the forefront of consideration. The third effect he calls obsolescence – aspects of the previous regime are rendered passé or even ridiculous. The fourth and final effect he calls reversal – operation of the new regime continues until its dysfunctionalities kick-in and change once again becomes necessary. This is a useful check for any change programme in any context, great for highlighting weaknesses and pointing up ways of putting them right. As he himself put it, 'there is absolutely no inevitability as long as there is a willingness to contemplate what is happening'. This is what makes trust analysis and the radical risk strategies that result, not only possible but also powerful and invigorating.

Marshall McLuhan and Quentin Fiore, produced by Jerome Agel, *The Medium is the Message: An Inventory of Effects*, Corte Madera: Gingko Press, 2001

Lewis H. Lapman, Introduction, in Marshall McLuhan, *Understanding Media: The Extensions of Man*, Cambridge, MA: MIT Press, 1994

Marshall McLuhan, Eric McLuhan and Frank Zingrone, *The Essential McLuhan*, New York: Basic Books, 1995

Index